W9-DJF-711

SVETOZAR KRALJEVIĆ • THE APPARITIONS OF OUR LADY AT MEĐUGORJE

INFORMATIVNI ✠ CENTAR
miv
M E Đ U G O R J E

FOR THE PUBLISHER:
Fr. Ivan Sesar

EDITOR:
Krešimir Šego

PREPARED FOR THE PRINT BY:
Jozo Kraljević

© Informativni centar "Mir" Međugorje

CIP – Katalogizacija u publikaciji
Nacionalna i univezitetska biblioteka
Bosne i Hercegovine, Sarajevo

27-312.47-587.6(497.6 Međugorje)

KRALJEVIĆ, Svetozar
    The apparitions of our Lady at Međugorje : a
historical account with interviews / Svetozar
Kraljević. 3th English ed. – Međugorje :
Informativni centar Mir, 2005. – 231 str. [24]
str. s tablama : ilustr. ; 20 cm

ISBN 9958-775-76-X

COBISS.BH-ID 14461702

Svetozar Kraljević O.F.M.

THE APPARITIONS OF OUR LADY AT MEĐUGORJE

A HISTORICAL ACCOUNT WITH INTERVIEWS

Third English Edition

INFORMATIVNI CENTAR "MIR" MEĐUGORJE
Međugorje, 2005.

DECLARATION OF THE AUTHOR

This book presents a truthful historical account of the extraordinary events that occurred at and near Međugorje, Bosnia and Herzegovina, since 1981. It does not anticipate in any way the judgment of the Church concerning the supernatural nature of those events. The author accepts the final decision of the Church's official investigation.

TABLE OF CONTENTS

PART 1
BEGINNINGS

PART 2
DEVELOPMENTS

PART 3
INTERVIEWS AND TESTIMONIES

PART 4
MISSION OF MEĐUGORJE FRIENDS

PART 5
DOCUMENTS AND EVALUATIONS

PREFACE

On March 5 and 6, 1983, I visited St. James parish in Međugorje, Herzegovina (B&H), and was present at the reported apparitions of Mary, the Mother of God, during the evening services on both days. I had decided to investigate these happenings after receiving the favorable reports of Father John Bertolucci and others who had visited the parish during December 1982. Father John, who lives with me at Holy Spirit Monastery, Bob Cavnar, a trustee of the University, and Jim Biegle, a student, presented film and testimonies that were very convincing.

During my visit to Međugorje, I was deeply impressed by the behavior of the visionaries, the reports of the parish priests and sisters, the response of the congregation and pilgrims, and the general, wholesome, spiritual atmosphere prevailing in the parish. I found the message important, powerful, and consistent with the gospels and the teaching of the Catholic Church. I could find no evidence that would motivate me to question the authenticity of the reports given by the six teenage visionaries.

The Church alone can make the final judgment on the truthfulness of the apparitions and the messages. The ecclesial investigations of the apparitions will undoubtedly be underway for an extended period of time. Meanwhile, I believe it is important to relate the facts of what has been said and heard in Međugorje. More importantly, I believe that the basic gospel message being proclaimed in terms of the events of our world today is a message that can make a decided and eternal difference in the lives of those who receive it. Many will recognize similarities in this message to that of the apparitions in Fatima, Portugal, in 1917. I hope none will miss the urgency in the call for peace, prayer, conversion, fasting, and penance. Here, as in Fatima, we are warned that a failure to respond will yield grave consequences.

May God be glorified in the response of His people to pursue true peace.

Holy Mary, Mother of God, Queen of Peace, pray for us.

Fr. Michael Scanlan, T.O.R.
President
The Franciscan University of Steubenville

April 1984

INTRODUCTION, 1983

For a group of children in the remote village of Međugorje, June 24,1981, was an ordinary, uneventful day. As they were walking in the surrounding mountains awaiting the next same kind of day to come, life took a new and unbelievable turn. When the children returned home, they spoke of an unusual experience of having seen Our Lady. Since then, this story of the children seeing Our Lady has already involved millions of people all over the world and for most of them life will never be the same. The apparitions long ago went beyond just a local importance and have become a global event biblically expressing the love of God for man and the thirst of man for God. No one had been able to foresee what the spirit of that first day would bring and who would be challenged by those words of the children. The years and events since 1981 have already clarified some things about the nature and the purpose of her call. Her message was about war and the thousands who would soon die and become refugees in the surroundings of Međugorje both in Croatia and Bosnia-Herzegovina.

In difficult times we often exclaim, "If I had only known!" The world was called to peace, but it went to war. Precisely ten years after Our Lady appeared, the first explosions of war were heard. We wonder what we shall miss again and what shall take place in the future?

This book will give only a limited insight into those events of the first days and some reflections that make no pretense of explaining everything. Every pilgrim traveling from far away, struggling on the journey, climbing the hills, and receiving the graces of sacraments will thereby become a participant in the very same events with his very own story.

Međugorje, St. Francis Feast, 1998.

Fra Svetozar Kraljević

INTRODUCTION, 2005

Before the evening service on June 24, 2005, Marija Pavlović-Lunetti said to Fr. Mario Knezović: **Father, she really does appear to us. She really does!** Now in 2005, Marija gives the same testimony and puts before us the same call as in 1981.

Since June 24, 1981, the unfolding world events, filled mostly with wars, speak of the nature of human hearts and the message of Our Lady.

Many say that the greatest event in their life is what took place on the hill of Podbrdo on June 24, 1981. Pilgrims believe that in this Christ-centered event Our Lady is present in the same way as in Cana of Galilee or at other places where she was with Jesus. As the servant of the Lord, she speaks the words of the Holy Spirit.

The presence of Our Lady meets the need and the thirst of human beings for God. Each person is filled with an intense desire for God and is in deep need for the supernatural. Humanity is curious about God. We are filled with the desire to be the person that we believe we are capable of being. We know that is possible only in God. This curiosity is expressed in love and faith, and for many, unfortunately, in hate and rejection.

Human beings appear confident, comfortable and self-sufficient and with no need for help from above. However, almost like in a secret conspiracy, unexpectedly, a person extends hands towards heaven and asks for the grace of faith to be rescued from the uncontrollable and threatening world. For this reason,

Međugorje remains a destination of so many who are seeking the face of God. Those who have been climbing the Međugorje mountains, who receive the sacraments and come again and again speak of the human thirst for Him.

Međugorje stands as an oasis in the desert. "Let anyone who thirsts come to me and drink" (Jn 7,37).

I offer this book to all those who want to seek answers to their life-questions, who face their need for and curiosity about God and who continue being pilgrims in their faith. Međugorje is a good place for all this to happen.

I wish to thank Wanda Rapacka, PHD, and Jozo Kraljević, BA, for their immeasurable help in publishing this book again.

Međugorje, the Feast Day of St. Bonaventura 2005.

Fra Svetozar Kraljević

THEOLOGICAL REFLECTION

Simple, faithful people readily accept and believe in apparitions and revelations (sometimes too readily or naively), but it is hard to find a solid work in the theological literature that is dedicated to these phenomena. Thus we tend to believe that Comte, the father of positivism, was correct when he said: "It (theology) will not occupy itself with God but with man; it will not search the unsearchable Truth, but the positive occurrences of its own community." In other words, theology's interest in God would be replaced by interest in man.

Also, because of many false reports of apparitions of Our Lady throughout the history of the Church, as well as fear that apparitions might remove Christ from the center of his mediating role in salvation – to say nothing of the demands of "ecumenism" – contemporary theology rarely approaches the subject of apparitions.

Nevertheless, this book runs counter to the bias of contemporary theology in its consideration of apparitions. For God, of course, is free to intervene in human history at any time. Theology, because it is in the service of the Church, must recognize God's salvific work in the world, which is always the continuation of what began in the Old Testament and was completed for all time in Jesus Christ. "Therefore the essence of all private revelations after Christ must be such as to fit into this eschatological salvific reality" (Karl Rahner, *Visionen und Prophezeiungen*, 1958, p. 26).

The Church is called to "put spirits to a test to see if they belong to God" (1 Jn 4:1) – or whether they turn the faithful from worshiping Jesus Christ and, instead, place Mary at the center of devotion, in competition with Christ.

This calling, therefore, also pertains to assessing the criteria of visionaries and their purported experiences.

Theology classifies apparitions in two categories: the mystical and the prophetic. The former is exclusively for the person in question, for his or her personal growth in the spiritual life.

The latter takes the form of a gift, to either an individual or a group, for the public benefit – for the benefit of the whole Church. Mystical apparitions are more intense and lead to a deeper spiritual experience of God, whereas prophetic apparitions do not necessarily have a strong influence on the person or persons; change is slower, in the sense of holiness of life.

For example, the revelation at Lourdes is authentic and is directed to the whole Church, but it is still, theologically considered, a "private" revelation and belief in it is not obligatory for the faithful – as distinguished from the "public" revelation contained in the Bible and the tradition of the Church, which is obligatory.

Logically, according to Karl Rahner, there is no difference in essence between private and public revelation (ibid., p. 24). In God, there is no "essential" and "less essential" revelation; every word from him is essential for the salvation of man. "The act of faith is connatural with the fact that God has spoken" (ibid.), publicly through Jesus Christ or privately through the prophet he has chosen.

The intent of private revelation is not to teach the faithful different meanings of existing truths; its imperative meaning is to help Christianity act in a particular historic situation (ibid., p. 27). The "matter" of private revelation is specific and practical advice that God directs to his Church when she finds herself in a situation where all other means are exhausted. Thus we conclude with Rahner: "Contrary to the fact that the revelation is ended, the prophetic element in the Church has its significance which cannot be substituted or replaced by the theological theory, human wisdom and understanding of the Church's teaching authority and mysticism" (ibid., p. 30). The Church would ignore this voice to her detriment.

When this voice is not completely clear, the Church, together with Mary, asks: "How can this be?" For Mary, certainty sprang from her candor and her obedience to God. The Church, in these circumstances, can only be open to the incentives of the Holy Spirit, while using all means for discernment of spirits.

How does one prove the authenticity of apparitions? The goal and the duty of investigation is to ascertain if such occurrences are products of the imagination and subjective experiences of the alleged visionaries. It cannot be presumed that visions are objective or "natural"; they must be proved. It must also be proved that the content of a vision and its formulation are beyond the grasp and abilities of the visionaries.

The greatest mistake, however, is to expect visionaries (if there are more than one) to relate their messages in exactly the same way. Subjectivity and differences in experiencing, receiving, transmitting, and explaining messages are not arguments against authenticity, but speak in its favor. To report a supernatural experience (such as a vision) "objectively," every individual must use his or her own expressions, metaphors, and descriptions. (See Rahner's *Privatoffenbarung*, 1963, p. 772). A good example of this is the Four Gospels, in which the mystery of Christ is presented in different ways.

(Most of these points were taken from an article "Ukazanja, Viđenja, Objave" written by Dr. prof. Ivan Dugandžić, who was a member of the first commission for investigation of the events in Međugorje, appointed by the bishop of Mostar, the Most Reverend Paul Žanić.)

Humac, 1983.

PART 1
BEGINNINGS

I

THE FIRST DAY

Međugorje ("between the hills") became known in Herzegovina and the world because of six young people who claim to have seen visions of Our Lady.

One of several villages in the area, Međugorje is the site of the parish church. The other villages are Bijakovići, Miletina, Vionica, and Šurmanci. The parish of Međugorje was mentioned in historical documents for the first time in 1599. It later disappeared from history, until 1892. The parish, which is in the care of Franciscans of the Province of Herzegovina, has about 730 families and belongs to the Diocese of Mostar. Now the parish has a new, large church, which was started in 1937 and finished in 1969.

One of the nearby hills, called Crnica, has another hill attached to it, called Podbrdo ("sub" or "under hill"), and the village of Bijakovići is at the base of the hill called Podbrdo. Podbrdo, between the larger hill, Crnica, and the village of Bijakovići, is the locale of the apparitions that are alleged to have started on June 24, 1981. Since that time, Podbrdo has become a place of pilgrimage and hope, and for others a "religious provocation."

Another hill, next to Crnica, was called Šipovac until 1933, when the parishioners built a large cross on it to mark and honor 1,900 years since the death of the Lord. The name of the hill was then changed to Križevac (*križ* in Croatian means "cross"). Since then, people from the parish and from the area have gathered there every year on the first Sunday after the feast of the Birth of Mary. In

21

1982, approximately 70,000 people gathered on the hill of Križevac.

Croatians came to Međugorje during the migration of peoples in the seventh century and soon thereafter received the Christian Faith, which has been firmly kept and severely tested ever since. In the Middle Ages, during the reign of the Croatian kings of Bosnia, Međugorje and all neighboring areas fell under the influence of the religious sect known as the Bogumils.

The Franciscans, who came to the area in the fourteenth century as missioners, preserved the Catholic Faith in Bosnia and Herzegovina, and the Holy See gave them the responsibility of being in that very difficult region in a very difficult time. The Turkish reign from 1478 to 1878, was a time of special trials and suffering. With great sacrifice – to which there are allusions in the Franciscan martyrologies – the Franciscans and the people lived, and survived, under Turkish-Muslim rule, and preserved their faith in God and their national identity.

Today, the new generations in Međugorje need not die for their faith, but they have to live for it and witness to it. For individuals, practicing the Faith – giving witness – means attending Sunday Mass, receiving the sacraments regularly, praying privately and in public, and providing their young with religious instruction. Nineteen priests and twenty nuns, all natives of Međugorje, work for the Church all over the world.

The bond of friendship between God and the people of Međugorje has endured for centuries. The rains of spring, the summer sun, the fruits of autumn, and the gentleness of the winter are divine benefactions to the land and the people – like a kiss imparted in times of trial and times of joy.

Hard work in this small, dry land, in its vineyards and tobacco fields – constant struggle in good times and bad – has taught these people persistence in their ways and their goals. Unfounded optimism has never carried them away, nor has pessimism impaired their zeal for life. The people accept new ways, however, if innovations promise to lead them better along their "old way" of faith in God and their sense of identity and community.

In ages past, they have been "rewarded" for their faith and loyalty with inequality, exile, degradation, poverty, and every form of humiliation. Therefore, their reasons for faith are held in their hearts, in their very being, deep in their souls. In the world where we live, we witness frequent changes in culture, attitudes, relationships – indeed, changes in almost everything. These people, however, change only when their faith in God and their individuality have been enhanced. We refer, of course, to their willingness to learn, to understand, and to make even better use of all of God's gifts.

In Međugorje, these people say that the six children who claim to have seen Our Lady are truthful. Because of this claim and the events that have followed, Međugorje has become a destination for hundreds of thousands of pilgrims from all over the world. Also scientists – experts in all areas of human interest – have come here. Many questions have been (and are) raised, as miracles happen and controversies abound. Pilgrims – that is, believers – look for consolation, hope, and peace, whereas nonbelievers see a "reactionary" movement. Many are searching for the deeper truth of the apparitions; others prefer to see them as a deception.

The first day of the visions and other unusual happenings in Međugorje was June 24, 1981 – the Feast of St. John the Baptist – and the "first" visionary was Ivanka Ivanković, who was born in Bijakovići, where the visions began. Ivanka and her parents go to Bijakovići often, where they have a house and property.

Mirjana Dragičević, the "second" visionary, lives in Sarajevo. Her parents moved from Bijakovići to Sarajevo before Mirjana was born, but she goes to Bijakovići every summer and stays with her grandmother. She spends most of her time in Bijakovići with local friends of her age, in the village or near it, which is also to say "close to nature."

There are no video arcades or similar places of entertainment for the young, as in large cities.

In an interview with me in February 1983, Ivanka spoke about the events of June 1981:

> We were together in my house, Mirjana and myself, and we went for a walk. When we were returning home, for some reason I looked toward the hill and saw a bright figure. I said, "Mirjana, look, the Madonna!" Mirjana waved her hand and said, "*Come on*! You think Our Lady would appear to us!" And we continued on our way home.

Later in that interview I asked Ivanka: "When you said 'Look, Our Lady!' did you say it to yourself or to Mirjana?" Ivanka answered: "To myself *and* to Mirjana, but I think more to myself than to Mirjana."

Further explaining what happened, Ivanka said:

> We came to Milka's house, in front of it, and Milka said: "Let us go to bring the sheep home." So we went there talking along the way. When we

arrived I saw Our Lady, holding Jesus in her hands, and then Mirjana and Milka looked and saw her.

On that same day, Vicka Ivanković, had taken the final examination of the school year (her "continuation" exam), and in the afternoon, because she was tired, she took a nap. While she was sleeping, but before they went on their walk to the hill, Ivanka and Mirjana left a message for Vicka with Vicka's mother, Zlata: "As soon as you get up come to Jakov's house." When Vicka awoke and got the message, she immediately went to Jakov's house, which Ivanka and Mirjana had already left, and then toward the place where she was told they would be.

In an interview with Fr. Tomislav Vlašić on March 15, 1982, Vicka recounted what had happened:

I went to look for Ivanka and Mirjana, because every summer we are together all the time. When I reached the road where they were, I noticed they were waving with their hands and calling me to come. I was wearing slippers. When I got to where they were, Mirjana said: "Look up there – Our Lady!" I said: "What do you mean, Our Lady? What is the matter with you?" I did not even look – did not take the time to bother to look.

I kicked off my slippers and ran barefooted, toward Čilići, along the macadam road. On my way back, I met Ivan Dragičević and Ivan Ivanković. They were picking apples, and asked me if I wanted some. I said no, and then I said: "Ivan (Dragičević), Our Lady – they said that Our Lady has appeared up there. Let's go there, you and me. I'm afraid." Ivan said: "Of course we'll go, but why are you afraid?" I thought: He's not afraid. But when we got there, and I turned toward Ivan and asked, "Do you see anything?" he was gone. I saw him running away.

Then I asked Ivan Ivanković: "Do you see anything?" He said: "I see something completely white, turning."

The little sister of Marija was with us then, and I asked her if she saw anything. She said: "I see Our Lady."

When I went up there the first time, I stood a little distance from them. I was afraid. But when I went the second time, I said to myself: If they are not running away, I will not run away either.

This was after 6:30 in the evening. It was raining a little and beginning to get dark.

I saw it – and what I saw was very white. I saw a gown, dark hair. All the time, she was covering and uncovering something she held in her left hand. I was not able to see what else she was doing, but it looked like she was showing something. Then she called to us to come closer – but who was going to get any closer? We were saying to each other: "She is calling us, but who is going to go?"

When I asked Vicka about the distance between Our Lady and the children, she said, "It was more than 200 meters." She also said:

I went home before the others. They remained there five or six minutes after me. Then I and little Milka went to Marija and told her that we had seen Our Lady on the hill. She just laughed and did not want to talk about it seriously. Then some people tried to tease us. "You should have caught her," Marija's uncle said. "Did she send greetings to your mothers and fathers?" My sister said: "Maybe they saw a flying saucer."

This is what happened the first time; but we did not pay any attention to what people said. We thought: Let them talk.

"Look, Our Lady!"

This statement, which Ivanka exclaimed immediately upon seeing the vision on the hill, was the first step on a journey of faith in Međugorje. We believe that this step was not taken on grounds of knowledge or intelligence, but inspiration, through the grace of God. Final judgment of the truthfulness of this description and of the visions at Međugorje has not yet been made by the Church. This writer, however, can no longer be impartial, or even pretend to be. I believe what the children say, what many people have experienced, and what I myself have heard and seen.

We would like these pages to say, in effect, "Look, Our Lady!" Nevertheless, every person – man, woman, and child – is free to choose what he will believe; is free to walk away; free to dismiss our contention with a wave of the hand; free to walk away, but also free to return, as Mirjana did, and look again   – despite fears and uncertainty.

Believers and nonbelievers, in short, are free to pray for guidance, free to change their beliefs, and free to search for more.

II

THE SECOND DAY

Although the apparition of Our Lady in Međugorje had the highest meaning and importance for many villagers and, especially, for the six children, everyone continued with the regular work in the fields – the same work that their predecessors performed for generations. Thus, on the second day of the apparitions, most of the visionaries were out in the fields, collecting tobacco leaves. They finished their work a little earlier than usual, whereupon Ivanka, Mirjana, Vicka, and Ivan Dragičević decided to return to the hill. In an interview with Fr. Tomislav Vlašić on March 15, 1982, Vicka said: "We decided to go. If we see her, that is okay. If we do not see her, what can we do?"

If Our Lady appeared, Vicka was to go to Marija Pavlović and Jakov Čolo and tell them to go to the hill. Marija and Jakov, however, had seen the three girls as they left the fields for the hill, and Marija had said to them: "If you see Our Lady, I would just like to be there. I do not have to see her." Two adults and some other children followed them to Podbrdo Hill, where they had seen the vision on the first day.

It was approximately 6:00 p.m. (Vicka told us). We went a little earlier. Mirjana and I were walking together, talking to each other. Ivanka was right in front of us. Suddenly she turned and said: "Look, Our Lady!" She saw her first. Then Mirjana and I looked where Ivanka had looked, and we both cried out: "Our Lady – it is she!"

It was still daylight and I was able to see her face, eyes, hair, and gown. I was able to recognize everything.

We were down on the road and did not know what to do. I went to call Marija and Jakov. They came immediately.

Milka, Marija's younger sister, did not go with the children on the second day because her mother had asked her to do some work in the field, and had told her: "Well, let Marija go; one is enough. Ivan Ivanković, who had seen the vision the first day, seemed to think that going to the hill to see some sort of "vision" was something only for children. He did not go the second day.

According to Vicka,

Our Lady called to us to go up on the hill, and we went. When you look up there from the bottom of the hill, it looks close, but it is not. We ran quickly up the hill. It was not like walking on the ground. Nor did we look for the path. We simply ran toward her. In five minutes we were on the hill – as if something had pulled us through the air. I was afraid. I also was barefoot, but no thorns had scratched me.

Those who watched the children run up the hill testify to the truthfulness of Vicka's words. They were amazed by the speed with which the children ran, and were not able to follow them to the top of the hill.

Vicka continued:

When we were about two meters away from Our Lady, we felt as if we were thrown to our knees. Jakov was thrown kneeling into a thorny bush, and I thought he would be injured. But he came out of it without a scratch.

Then I asked: "Marija, do you see Our Lady?" She said: "I see something white; it is getting clearer." Later she saw, like the rest of us.

Jakov said: "I see Our Lady" but Ivanka talked to her first. Her mother had died two months earlier, and Ivanka asked about her. Our Lady told Ivanka that her mother is well, is with her, and that Ivanka should not worry. Because her mother had died in the hospital and no one was with her, Ivanka had wondered if she had left a message for her children. Our Lady answered, "Obey your grandmother and be good to her because she is old and cannot work."

In a further report to Fr. Tomislav, Vicka said:

Mirjana complained to Our Lady. "Dear Our Lady, they will not believe us when we go home. They will tell us that we are crazy." Our Lady just smiled.

We were on the hill for ten to fifteen minutes. Meanwhile, some people had come up to join us. When we were about to leave, Our Lady seemed to be hovering in the air, and we didn't know what to say. Then she said to us: "Go in God's peace." Our heads were all turned in the direction where she was leaving – all in the same direction. No one said anything, but everyone was frightened.

Fr. Tomislav asked her: "Why did you start praying seven Our Fathers and the Credo?" and Vicka answered:

When we were on the hill, praying with Our Lady on the second day, we prayed seven Our Fathers. We were praying because we did not know what else to do. We were crying a little and praying a little. Later, she told us to pray seven Our Fathers, Hail Marys, Glorias, and the Credo.

Two facts or considerations are very important in analyzing the events of the second day: (1) Later, Our Lady wanted this day to be remembered as the day of her apparition, and (2) A permanent body of visionaries was formed on this day.

The members of the group are Ivanka Ivanković, Mirjana Dragičević, Vicka Ivanković, Marija Pavlović, Ivan Dragičević, and Jakov Čolo. Since the second day of the apparition until Christmas Day, December 25, 1982, all of these six persons have claimed to have had visions of Our Lady every day at about six o'clock every evening. Although Mirjana Dragičević says that December 25, 1982, was the last day of her visions of Our Lady, all the others still claim to see this vision.

III

THE THIRD DAY

By the third day, the news of the apparitions had spread far beyond Bijakovići, and several thousand people gathered on the hill. These people came from villages in the area – Miletina, Čitluk, Ljubuški, and from even greater distances.

Marinko Ivanković, a neighbor of the children and a sincere, practicing Christian, became a member of the children's group, not as a visionary but as an organizer, protector, supporter, and adult leader or advisor.

On this third day, the children, with Marinko, decided to meet at the bottom of the hill below the site of the first apparition. The appearance of Our Lady was preceded on the third day by a brilliant light that shone on the village and the entire area. Fr. Jozo, in an interview on June 28, 1981, asked Jakov:

> "Are you able to find the spot for the apparition by yourselves or are you led to the spot by, as it were, a special sign?" "I wouldn't be able to find the spot on my own (Jakov answered). We see a light that surrounds Our Lady, and follow wherever the light and Our Lady move."

People in the village who also have seen this light believe that it indicates the place where Our Lady appears to the children. They interpret it as a message to the children – "Come here; I am here!" – and also to all others: "Come! This is a special place. Something special is happening here." Every apparition on the hill has been preceded by this unusual light.

In an interview with me on February 27, 1983, Marinko Ivanković discussed all the events that he was a close witness of, and talking about the third day, he said:

> The others said: "See the light! See Our Lady!" This third evening, Our Lady was about 300 meters farther away from the place where she had appeared the first two evenings... The children told me where to go, and besides, I know the hill very well, so I knew how to get there; and we climbed higher on the hill. I had taken the holy water from my house, to sprinkle it around the vision, in order to see what she is: whether Our Lady or a devil. However, when we had climbed up the hill, we knelt down, and I gave the holy water to Vicka to sprinkle. She said: "If you are Our Lady, stay with us. If you are not, be gone!"

The children reported that Our Lady smiled beautifully on them after they had tested her. They understood her smile as indicating her pleasure at having secured their faith in her presence.

Feeling among the children and the people was high. It can be described as an emotional response, as well as a religious feeling, of the highest kind. Everybody wanted to be a close witness of everything that happened. Typical of the season in this region, the summer heat was intense, and seemed even worse because of the immense crowds of people.

The children, whom the pilgrims were able to see, and Our Lady, whom the pilgrims were not able to see, were the center of attention, to whom every person wanted to be close. Every thought, every movement, every eye seemed directed upon the visionaries, so that, together with the heat, the pressure and demands of the pilgrims became almost unbearable. Indeed, Ivanka and Mirjana succumbed to a prolonged faint and had to be secluded and revived.

On this third day, the vision lasted approximately thirty minutes. After ten minutes, Our Lady told the children: "Stand. Do not kneel anymore."

In the March 3, 1982 interview in Međugorje between Vicka and Fr. Tomislav, Vicka related the events of the third day and the message of Our Lady.

Fr. Tomislav: When you were on the hill the third day, was there anything special about what happened, or was it much the same as the second day?

Vicka: The third day we asked questions. We had been told to ask her what her name was and why she had come to our village.

T: What did she say?

V: She said: "I am the Blessed Virgin Mary." She also said: "I came here because there are many devout believers here. I have come to convert and reconcile people."

T: You said that her first message was a call for peace.

V: Yes... but the first, second, third, and fourth days have got mixed up. Anyway, I know that on one of those days she said that her most important message is to call the world to peace.

T: Well, how did you understand that call to peace – for the whole of mankind or just for individuals?

V: I thought that she was calling for peace for mankind. If she had said: Reconcile among yourselves, that would mean something else.

T: She actually told you she'd appeared so as to call the world to peace?

V: Yes.

T: What other messages did she give?

V: Her main message is that she calls the world to peace, conversion, prayer, and penance.

Jakov, in an interview with Fr. Jozo on June 28, 1981, was more specific about Our Lady's message of peace on the third day. "We asked (Jakov said): 'Dear Our Lady, why have you come to us?' She said: 'I have come because there are many believers here!' Then she said that all are to be at peace, that all are to be reconciled."

In their reporting, the children's versions are slightly different from each other's when they quote Our Lady – as we see between Vicka and Jakov. These differences, however, are in their wording, not in the basic meaning.

As I searched for information and facts about this apparition of the Blessed Virgin Mary, I feared that I might be overlooking a very important dimension of the communications between Our Lady and the visionaries. Prayer is the visionaries' most important mode of communication with Our Lady, in the visions and in their daily lives. The basic content of the vision of the third day – as in any vision on any day – was prayer, in the form of reciting words and singing hymns, as well as in just being there.

The children asked Our Lady if she would come again, and she answered: "I will come again to the old place. Go in God's peace."

The children and the people began to leave the hillside. Marija walked toward the village with some women, and suddenly, Our Lady reappeared and Marija dropped to her knees. Later, Marija said she had seen a bare cross, formed of all colors of the rainbow but without a corpus, and in front of the cross, in tears, was Our Lady, urging: "Peace, peace, only peace. Reconcile yourselves. Peace must take place between God and man and between men." Her final words were: "Go in God's peace."

The Local People and the New Times

The people of the parish of Međugorje, and especially the people of the village of Bijakovići, have been affected by the visions in the deepest, most profound manner. On the third day, and ever since, pilgrims – from the region and from all over the world – have experienced the love and hospitality of the local people, who have become the most outspoken witnesses to the truthfulness of the visions. This shows when there is a need for patience with the pilgrims who want a drink of water or want merely to ask questions, or, according to the times, when pilgrims and non-pilgrims alike must withstand severest pressures.

The youthful visionaries, together with the priests, nuns, and parishioners (but especially the families of the children), have been given special roles to play in this drama of the apparition of the Blessed Virgin. This is true also for people in the government. Many lives, many souls, many minds have been moved.

When Fr. John Bertolucci and Mr. Bob Cavnar came to Međugorje to film a television program, they asked Our Lady, through the children, if the television crew would be able to travel through to Međugorje. (They were in

Rome awaiting government clearance to enter the country.) Our Lady answered: "It will be difficult but all will be for the glory of God." We, in turn, assert the same judgment for everything that has happened in Međugorje: There are difficulties, and times to be patient; there are times to be ready to suffer. But everything is for the greater glory of God.

IV

THE FOURTH DAY

On the fourth day of the apparitions, Saturday, June 27, the local government authorities in Čitluk became interested in the events in the parish of Međugorje, and summoned the six children for investigation that afternoon. During interrogation at the police station, the children remained firm in their contention that they had seen Our Lady. Then they were sent to be examined by the doctor on duty, Dr. Ante Vujević.

Dr. Vujević, a general practitioner, first examined – for more than one hour – Ivan Dragičević. Vicka was to be examined next, but by then the time of the vision was drawing near and the children wanted to return to the hill to see Our Lady. Vicka stayed in the doctor's office only a short time and at 5:45 the five of them (except Ivan) left the office, got a taxi, and returned to the hill. (Ivan was taken home by a relative a little later.)

Dr. Vujević had not found anything amiss in his examination, but is on record as saying: "It is not within my competence to make a final judgment." Later, Dr. Vujević refused to become involved in investigations of the visions because of strong public love and support for the children. "I do not want to come out of this in the public's eyes as an atheist or anything like that," he said. "My private conviction will remain private."

Darinka Glamuzina, a doctor with the ambulance squad in Čitluk and a self-proclaimed atheist, was sent to the site of the apparitions to investigate. The testimony of those who saw her, as she came down the hill after the vision, is that she had been severely shocked by something. Later, she would have nothing more to do with the investigations. It is not known whether she became a believer, but those who saw her on the fourth day believe she had an unusual experience.

On this day, the children had separated into three groups: Ivanka, Marjana, and Vicka; Marija and Jakov; and Ivan. Marija and Jakov were accompanied on their way to the hill by Fr. Zrinko Čuvalo, the associate pastor from the parish, who asked to stay close to them so that he might be better able to observe the happenings. This was the first time that a priest accompanied either the children or the people to the site of the visions.

When Fr. Zrinko and Marija reached the place on the road at the bottom of the hill of the first-day vision, Marija saw a special light. She understood the light as a call, directing her, and ran, with great speed, to where it beckoned – oblivious of Fr. Zrinko and everything else. Fr. Viktor Kosir was nearby at that moment, but neither priest was able to follow Marija as she ran up the hill. When Marija had climbed approximately 20 meters higher than the place at which Our Lady had appeared on the second day, Our Lady was standing in front of her, then disappeared, all the while remaining perfectly silent.

Marija was unable to see the other visionaries because of the crowd of people around her. They had lost sight of each other in the multitude. Jakov, however, found Ivanka, Mirjana, and Vicka – and together they found Marija, who seemed to be waiting for something, not knowing what to do. Reunited, they began to pray – Our Father, Hail Mary, and Glory Be – then sing. All the people on the hillside joined in the praying and singing.

The children had a strong feeling that Our Lady would return, and she did. Those who were nearby could tell from the strange expression on the children's faces that something unusual was happening, and they pushed toward the place where they thought Our Lady was standing. The people seemed to have no control over their emotions or their movements. They seemed to have a glimpse of the strange light, but were not able to see Our Lady. By looking at the children and their eyes, they could tell where she was standing. Everybody tried to get closer – to see, to touch, to experience. The children saw that the crowd was treading upon the Virgin's long veil, and told them not to, but by now the crowd was beyond control. Again, Our Lady disappeared.

Some of the people tried to be more orderly by standing in a circle around the children, but when Our Lady reappeared, a boy stepped on her veil (according to Marija's testimony) and again she disappeared. The next time Our Lady appeared, the people in the circle were more orderly, and the apparition lasted longer.

When Our Lady seemed to have reappeared, then disappeared for the last time, she left without saying her usual words at parting, "Go in God's peace." Taking note of this omission, the children prayed at length, in the hope that she would soon reappear, but when, at last, she did not, finally everyone began to leave the hill.

As we follow the events we notice an interesting variation. On the second, third, and fourth days, Our Lady appeared at different places. The various sites of the apparitions had no significance for the children: they had always followed a light that led them to Our Lady; and for many, this was sufficient evidence of the apparitions' authenticity. The fact that the children were not restricted to a particular site, but followed the light wherever it led, contributed to the likelihood of the apparitions.

Also on this fourth day, the children asked Our Lady several questions. Fr. Jozo had asked if Our Lady had something to say to priests, and Our Lady said: "Let them believe strongly and guard their faith!" Vicka asked Our Lady to prove to those present that she is there. Our Lady said, "Let those who do not see believe as if they see."

Mirjana was greatly concerned by allegations of skeptics, who attributed the visions to the hallucinations of drug addicts or epileptics – and especially to herself. When she expressed this concern, Our Lady told her: "There is always injustice among people. Pay no attention to what such people say." Mirjana, and all the other children, were greatly consoled by this. When Ivanka asked Our Lady her name, she responded, "I am the Blessed Virgin Mary."

Our Lady told the children, "You are my angels, my dear angels," and promised she would return the next day.

In their concern, Ivan's parents had asked him to stay home on this fourth day; so Ivan had not gone to the hill. The major reason for the parents' concern was fear of the police, who were keeping watch on these happenings in Međugorje, and harassment by them. Later, in formal testimony, Ivan said he had had severe stomach cramps but nevertheless was despondent that he had not made the trek to the hill. He decided, moreover, that "I will never be absent again!" (Our Lady had noticed his absence and asked: "Where is that boy?")

Although Ivan did not go to the hill that day, he had gone a short distance from the village in that direction, and by the side of the road Our Lady appeared to him. Asked about the content of this apparition, he said: "She greeted me, told me to be at peace, and departed with a cheerful goodbye smile on her face."

These details of the happenings of the fourth day are mostly from Marija's testimony, which was given to Fr. Jozo the next day, Sunday, June 28. When Fr. Jozo asked her, "How did you feel? Did you feel a joy in your heart?" she said: "There is just no way I can describe my great, great joy when I see her!"

V

THE FIFTH DAY

The fifth day was a sunny Sunday. Word about the apparitions had spread throughout the area. People from neighboring villages, parishes, and counties came to Bijakovići to witness the happenings. It was estimated that more than 15,000 people had gathered outside Bijakovići that Sunday when the children arrived at the site of the visions, a little after six in the evening. The sun was still bright and hot. Except for the dialogue during the vision that day, a local person Grgo Kozina was able to tape-record every word the children spoke to the crowd, as they asked questions of Our Lady and repeated her answers to the people. At exactly 6:30, Our Lady appeared to the children, and they asked the people to kneel.

Children: Dear Our Lady! What do you wish from us (i.e., the children)?

Our Lady: Faith and respect for me.

C: Dear Our Lady! What do you wish from our priests?

M: That they firmly believe.

C: Dear Our Lady! Why don't you appear in the church so that everybody sees you?

M: Blessed are they who have not seen and believe.

C: Dear Our Lady! Will you come again? (She will; she will come to the same place. She will come.) Dear Our Lady! Which do you like better: that we pray to you or sing to you?

M: Do both: sing and pray.

C: Dear Our Lady! What do you wish from these people who have gathered here? (At this point, the children said, Our Lady, before she answered: "Looked at all the people and smiled.")

M: Let them believe as if they see.

C: She is disappearing. She is gone.

The above dialogue took place between 6:30 and 6:40 p.m. Then Vicka said: "We will pray again. She did not say anything to us." (I.e., she did not say: "Go in God's peace.") The children then prayed two Our Fathers, two Hail Marys, and two Glorias.

C: There she is again! Let us sing a song! (Marija began to sing a song: "Marijo, Marijo, o kako lijepa si...")

M: My Angels, my dear angels!

C: Dear Our Lady! What do you wish from these people here?

M: Let these people, who do not see me, believe the same as the six of you, who see me.

C: Dear Our Lady! Will you leave us some sign, here on earth, so that we can convince people that we are not liars, that we do not lie, that we do not play games with you?

M: Go in God's peace!

C: She left! There's a light behind her! She is gone!

The children then sang well-known Croatian religious songs: "Sred te se pećine," "Marijo, O Marijo," "Kriste, u tvoje ime." Then the tape ends.

Immediately after this vision, Fr. Zrinko Čuvalo subjected the children to extremely harsh questioning and, sometimes not letting them answer, asked even more questions, trying to undermine everything they said and to lead them to make contradictory statements. His questions served his purpose well, but did not daunt the children. On paper in black and white, his questions (below) do not have the same vigor and sting as when they were asked, aloud and directly, in the original language.

When I asked Fr. Zrinko about this interrogation, he explained that he was purposefully antagonistic, playing devil's advocate by asking apparently hostile questions – in effect, directly opposite to what he had witnessed during the vision. For example, he had asked Vicka: "Why didn't you say 'There she is!'?" although he had heard her say exactly that.

Fr. Zrinko: Please – any two of you – what did you talk about to each other?

Ivanka: Three of us were talking about the questions we would ask her.

Z: Did Ivanka or Vicka whisper something to you?

Jakov: Neither one whispered anything to me!

Z: Tell me! Did you see anything this evening?

Vicka: I did!

Z: Tell me! Why didn't you say "There she is!" as you cried out the other night, when you say you saw her the first time?

V: I did say that!

Z: You did not!

V: I did!

Z: I did not hear it – and I was right in front of you!

V: What are you saying? I told them that!

Z: Good! Good! (To Marija:) Did Vicka whisper anything to you?

Marija: She did not!

Z (to Ivan): Did you see anything this evening?

Ivan: I did!

Z: You did? What did you see?

I: I looked there, and there she was!

Z: When you saw her, why didn't you say "There she is!"? Jakov! Did Ivanka whisper anything to you?

J: She did not!

Z; How about Vicka?

J: She did not! Nothing!

Z: Did you see anything?

J: I did!

Z: What did you see?

J: I saw Our Lady!

Z: When you saw her, why didn't you say "There she is!"?

J: I did not...

Z: Good! Good!

Fr. Zrinko Čuvalo is now a firm believer in the truthfulness of the apparitions in Međugorje, and although he is now associate pastor in Posuški Gradac, he returns to Međugorje as often as possible. The message of Our Lady has become his way of life.

The Words of the Holy Father

After I listened to the tape recording of the conversations of the fifth day, I turned the tape on the other side and found a speech of the Holy Father, John Paul II, to Croatian pilgrims who had traveled to Rome in 1979 to celebrate the 1,300 years since Croatians had come to the region where they now live and the 1,000 years since the

Croatian king, Branimir, had been baptized with all his people. (The tape was made from the program of Vatican Radio.)

Speaking to the pilgrims, John Paul had mentioned the "threefold fidelity" of the Croatian people, to our Lord Jesus Christ and to the Holy See of St. Peter, and then he said:

> The third aspect of your fidelity is the love and devotion of the Croatian people to the Blessed Virgin Mary, the Mother of the Church, whom you most dearly call "Queen of the Croatians" and whom you honor in numerous shrines, so that you transform this threefold fidelity into your centuries-old great pledge of fidelity to Jesus Christ, the Church, and the Mother of God.

It was by such a coincidence that I found this speech of John Paul II, speaking in Croatian to Croatians and re-minding them of their fidelity to God, of the great tradition of family prayer, and respect for life. Indeed, I thought, these people of Međugorje had heard this message recently, from the Holy Father, who repeated the words of Jesus Christ in the Gospel, and again, even more recently, as spoken just the other day by Mary in Međugorje.

VI

THE SIXTH DAY

On the sixth day, Monday, the children were again summoned to Čitluk by the authorities, and then sent to Mostar, to the neuropsychiatric department of the Dr. Safet Mujić Hospital. It was expected that the six children would be declared mentally ill, or hallucinatory, etc. In thorough examinations, however, they passed every test and answered all questions without guile or hesitation, so that Dr. Mulija Džudža declared them sound and healthy.

That evening, after they returned home, the children had another vision of the Blessed Virgin.

The day was still hot and sunny, and the crowd on the hillside joined the children in praying – Our Father, Hail Mary, and the Gloria. Then they sang "Sred te se pećine" and "Marijo, O Marijo," and were singing "Kriste! U tvoje ime," when, at 6:26, the Virgin appeared. The Virgin's words could not be heard directly by the people or tape-recorded, and therefore are not reproduced below. The following are the children's words, spoken directly to the Virgin or relayed by them to the people on the hillside, as recorded by Grgo Kozina, one of the local people.

K: They just knelt.

Children: Dear Our Lady! Are you glad that the people are here? (She is smiling. She is glad.) Dear Our Lady! How many days will you stay with us?

Our Lady: As long as you wish.

C: Will you leave us a sign?

M: I will come again tomorrow.

C: Dear Our Lady! What do you wish that these people do?

M: There is only one God and one faith. Believe firmly!

C: Will we be able to endure all this? Many people persecute us because we "see."

M: You will endure, my angels.

C: Dear Our Lady! What wish do you have for us here?

M: That you have firm faith and confidence.

C: Dear Our Lady! Could this lady (Dr. Darinka Glamuzina) touch you?

M: There have always been unfaithful Judases. Let her come.

C: She is touching her. She left! She left! (The children resumed singing with the people: "Sred te se pećine" and "Marijo, O Marijo.")

C: The light! The light! Here she is! Here she is! Dear Our Lady! Will this little boy, Daniel, ever be able to speak? Please make a miracle so that everyone will believe us. These people love you very much. Dear Our Lady! Make one miracle. (She is looking at him.) Dear Our Lady! Say something.

K: Is she still looking at the boy?

C: (She is looking at the boy, who is mute, dumb.) Dear Our Lady! Say something, we ask you. Say something, we ask you. Say something, dear Our Lady!

M: Let them (Daniel's parents) firmly believe that he will be healed. Go in God's peace.

C: She has left. Look, the light!

The singing continued ("Kriste, u tvoje ime"). Immediately after the vision when they were asked about the messages, the children repeated what Our Lady had said during the vision.

VII

THE SEVENTH DAY
The Vision in Cerno

On the seventh day there were new developments that are especially important both for that day and for later events at Međugorje. Because of the great number and complexity of details, we have abbreviated the conversation between the pastor, Fr. Jozo Zovko, and five of the visionaries, which was recorded immediately after the apparition on this day. The sixth child, Ivan Dragičević, was not at the site of the vision, nor did he see a vision, and he was not present at this conversation. Parts of the conversation have been omitted and sentences and fragments of sentences have been combined, but nothing has been added.

When Fr. Jozo began the conversation, he thought the children's seventh-day vision had been at the same site as on the previous days, not knowing that they had been taken by social workers to nearby cities and villages (Čitluk, Počitelj, Čapljina, the waterfall of Kravica, and Cerno, where they arrived at the usual time of the apparitions). Moreover, thousands of people were waiting for them on the hillside in Bijakovići.

Fr. Jozo: Ivanka, tell us what happened.

Ivanka: First, we prayed our usual prayers. Then, not thinking about what I was doing, I looked up the hill and saw a light and the light was coming toward us. On the hillside where the people were, they – and everything – were bathed in the light. Those two girls (who had driven them on the trip) saw this. I said: "Do you see the light?" They said: "We see it." I looked at the light all the time. Then we knelt and sang.

J: Mirjana, what did you talk about with Our Lady?

Mirjana: I asked her if she was displeased that we had left the hill and gone to the other place. She said that she does not mind.

J: Where did you go?

M: Cerno. We left a sign or a mark where we were. Then we asked if she minds if we do not go the hill anymore and, instead, to the church. Somehow, she seemed undecided when we asked her this. Even so, she said that she will not mind.

I: It (the apparition) will be at the same time.

J: Did you ask those questions?

M: No, we did not have them with us. We were eating when Vicka told us that some police inspectors would come and that we should go to another place to see if the Virgin would appear to us in a different place. So we dressed in a hurry and left the written questions behind in our other clothes. We were in a hurry. We ran to the car and left quickly.

I: We asked if she would leave us some sign. She slowly moved away, and the light appeared on the hill again where the people were.

M: And she said: "Go in God's peace!"

Jakov: She also said "My angels." When we asked if she would mind appearing to us in the church, she said: "I will not, my angels."

M: For a long time she looked at us, like...

Jozo: Well, what did you say to the people on the hill?

All: We did not go to the hill!

I: We were in Cerno, close to Ljubuški. We could see the hill from there.

J: You were in Cerno?

All: Yes, in Cerno!

J: Why did you go there when the people were here?

V: Because the inspectors took us to another place to see if she would appear there, too.

J: When was that inspection made? You were here, and yet you did not say anything about it.

All: Today, around two o'clock.

J: Is the other place a good place? Is it similar to here?

I: Yes, it is the same!

J: Were there any people with you?

V: Nobody! We were alone with these two girls. They saw the light shining on the hill.

A new dilemma that arose from this conversation was whether the children should go to the hill where the people were waiting for them to have the next vision. They debated whether they should tell the people that the vision had been at another site and what Our Lady had said to them. Because the crowd had become immense, the children were urged not to show themselves publicly that day.

Jozo: Mirjana, what would you say to the people? They are still waiting on the hill.

M: Something urges me to go on the hill. Something seems to be telling me to say: "Our Lady has appeared at another place. She told us we should go to the church for visions." We should say that all true Christians should go to the church.

J: Then go and tell the people!

V: Father, don't do that. They (the police inspectors) told us not to go there until all the people leave, after nine o'clock. They told us: "If you want to go to the church

and make fools of yourselves, you shouldn't allow
yourselves to make fools as well of people who would
follow you there. Keep out of sight. The people are
walking off their jobs. Nobody wants to do anything.
Everyone thinks only of seeing you."

J: But if Our Lady has told you that you should inform the
people of something, how can you dare not to – if she
was Our Lady?

V: I won't be unfair to anyone. I will tell the people. I
know that the people will come again, and the word
will spread. I will tell everybody I see.

I: Let someone else speak to the people.

J: We can't become involved in this, because we haven't
seen anything.

V: You didn't understand me, Father. We spoke to the
people last night, from Marinko's terrace. We repeated
everything Our Lady had told us. And we could not be
happier. We are always happy. The people did not
leave us until eleven o'clock. We told them everything
we knew, but nothing is enough.

J: Do you agree that the people should come to the church
tomorrow?

All: We do!

J: What if the people do not come to the church?

V: That will be okay. It would be better if the six of us
were alone. We would prefer that nobody comes,
Father. It would be better for us, I'm sure.

J: Does Our Lady come because of you or because of the
people?

I: Because of us. Why did she choose us?

Mar.: I think because of us and because of the people,
equally.

Mir.: I think because of us and because of the people, to
strengthen the faith of the people. She said: "Reconcile

the people!" I have strong sympathy for the people.
They did not come here to waste their time.

V: If we go out to the people and try to talk to them, they
will think – who knows what they will think? They
will say: "Where were they when they should have
been here?" Who knows what they might say! Those
who believe in God know what is of God, and will
learn everything that they have to know. However they
found out about all this the first time, they'll find out
the same way again. Everyone who believes will come
again. And we know very well why the unbelievers
come – to make fun of Our Lady or to curse her – or to
make a fuss so that nobody can hear a word. I know
this for a fact!

Vicka's statement (above), that she would tell everyone she met the message of Our Lady, is, as it turned out,
the crux of the situation and vital testimony to the events
of that day and the early days. On that day, Vicka
formulated the invitation of all pilgrims to the church.

Another important, though controversial, aspect of the
day was the children's contention that Our Lady had told
them that she would return for only three more days, until
Friday (July 3, 1981).

In my interview with Father Jozo Zovko, held on
August 11, 1983, I asked him if he could explain the
statement, which proved to be wrong. He explained that
he had asked the children to deepen their faith, had given
them the Bible to read, and had asked them to pray. He
also gave them a book about Lourdes, which they all read.
From the number of apparitions to Bernadette at Lourdes
(nineteen), the children concluded that they would have
the same number of apparitions, and had come to him and

said, "Friday will be our last day." They were counting all the apparitions from Wednesday, June 24 to Tuesday, June 30, and there were sixteen of them.

Some witnesses believe that the children, harried and besieged by masses of curious pilgrims, as well as by those whose motives were selfish or indifferent sought to reduce the tensions upon them by saying: "She will appear until Friday."

Regardless, we do know that Our Lady continued to appear to the children. On Saturday, the children had not come together. Ivan was at his house, Vicka was picking flowers and Marija was at home. Vicka said, "When the time came my hands were stiffened. I fell to my knees." Marija relates, "I was home thinking that Our Lady will not come again. I was entering my room and I saw Our Lady. I fell to my knees. Ante, who was behind me, ran away. I stayed there alone, praying. Later, I told the others, 'Our Lady was with me.' They had all seen her also. So Sunday, we got together and she came. We concluded that this is not like Lourdes."

On the evening of this seventh day, following their report of the events of the day, the children returned to Bijakovići where they learned that Marinko Ivanković had been taken to the police station for interrogation. Even though it was around 10 o'clock in the evening, they decided to go to the police to testify that Marinko had not initiated the visions and that he was guilty of nothing.

The hardships, trials, fear, and pain endured by the visionaries and their parents that night were all a part of the mission for which they had been called. God continued to pour out his graces, pilgrims continued to journey to Međugorje and recognize these special manifestations of the Lord.

VIII

THE EIGHTH DAY

In their report of the vision in Cerno, the children revealed the invitation to the people to gather in the church. Father Jozo Zovko, in an interview with me on August 11, 1983 spoke about what was, for him, the first sign from God which led him to believe in the apparitions. I asked Father Jozo what happened next.

Jozo: "I was in anguish because of all the events. It was at this time that something began to happen in me which led me to become more than just a listener to the children's reports.

People from the government service were brought in to put a stop to the events. Those who were believers did not do it happily. The two girls who had experienced the events in Cerno resigned because of their own experience. The police came to intervene directly. Someone came to Vicka's mother and said, 'Zlata, let the children go no more to the church, let the children give that up. It is going to be difficult for you.'

Zlata answered, 'I will see. I do not know. Who can order a child what to do?'

Sometime in the middle of the day the police came to find the children, to try to stop them after the two girls had failed. They wanted to remove them from the hill and from the people. They asked throughout the village where the children were. The people responded in various ways; in the fields, in the village, here, there. Meanwhile, the children, who knew they were being sought, were running from the village through the vineyards, toward the church.

In the process of escaping, they even changed their clothes in order to change their appearance. It was like playing a game of hide and seek.

While all this was going on, I was in the church praying, feeling great responsibility in front of God as pastor. The people were asking questions and I had to say something to the people, to the priests and the sisters. In a way, I felt like Moses before the Red Sea and I knew that I could speak only to God. No man could have answered my need. I prayed, 'God, I know you talked to Abraham, to Moses and to others. Now there are thousands of people here these days. Tell me where the river is going. I do not know where the mouth of that river is, nor what its source is.'

No one was in the church with me at that moment. And then, something happened that for me was important and decisive. It was both a turning point and a moment of revelation. While I was praying, I heard a voice say, 'Come out and protect the children.' I left my Bible and breviary, genuflected and with no further thought nor delay left the church. As I was leaving the church through the middle door, with my foot still in the air and the door handle in my hand, the children ran toward me from the left side of the church, escaping from the police. They told me, 'The police are chasing us. Hide us.' They had gathered around me and were crying. Ana, Vicka's sister, was with them, sharing their fate. I embraced the children and took them to the rectory. I locked them in an unoccupied room of the house.

Soon the police came. They asked me, 'Did you see the children?' 'I did,' I answered. The police kept running very fast toward the village of Bijakovići to catch them. After the police left, I went to talk with the children. I asked them to stay in the rectory so they would not be caught. Shortly after Our Lady came to them in the room. Later there were seven visions in that same room."

Sometime later in the afternoon word got to the pilgrims who were going to the hill that there would be a service in the church. Around 5:00 p.m. Father Zrinko Čuvalo, the associate pastor, led the prayer of the Rosary and at 6:00, Father Jozo, the pastor, celebrated Mass.

Of this first evening Mass, Father Jozo commented, "There is nothing to which I could compare the number of people in the church. It was so crowded that I found it impossible to extend my hands and say, 'The Lord be with you.' In the homily I asked the people to pray and to fast, begging God to help us to understand the events in our parish. That mass of people responded to my request with a great exclamation, full of faith, 'We will.'"

I asked Father Jozo what led him to start the Mass in conjunction with the apparitions. He responded, "My motives were based on the value of the Mass. I would have nothing even close in its value to offer to the people gathered there. In that Mass, I wanted the people to cease being spectators and become participants in the events."

In reality, this is what has happened. The spectators became the participants. The experience of the children, the visionaries, in a very special way becomes the experience of the pilgrims, as they come to the church, pray the Rosary and join in the celebration of Mass.

PART 2
DEVELOPMENTS

IX

APPARITIONS IN THE CHURCH, RECTORY, FIELDS, AND HOMES

After the eighth day, the Virgin appeared several times in the rectory of the parish church of Međugorje. Subsequently however, sites and dates become uncertain, although the apparitions continued on a daily basis. Also, after July 3 we do not know the specific conversation of each apparition.

Because of the large crowds, the site of the apparitions settled on the hillside, where the Virgin continued to appear daily – until August 12, 1981 when the officials decreed that the hillside was off limits to everyone. Accordingly, the children moved the site to their village of Bijakovići, to the woods and fields. At times, the site was the home of one of the children, where everyone gathered to pray and await Our Lady.

Together with Our Lady, the children formed a prayer group, and besides instructing them, she joined them in singing and praying. Fr. Janko Bubalo, who followed the events very closely, told me: "Most of the messages for the people were delivered there in the fields." The image struck me most forcefully: Our Lady and her loving children at ease in our fields! Still, one cannot but be moved by the image of the Virgin deprived of even a barren spot on earth: a desolate hillside!

Apparitions in the Parish Church

For pastoral reasons, the attitude of parishioners, and overall developments, the children were asked to "arrange" to have their visions in the church. Although these visions have continued in the church ever since, there were, in all, five days when the apparition failed to occur, which saddened the children greatly. This indicates, however, that neither the children – nor anyone else – have power to set conditions for the apparitions. From day to day, no one knows whether there will be an apparition. It cannot be known in advance that Our Lady will appear or not appear. Thus God himself chooses the days it will happen.

Evening Services

Those who have been in Međugorje since the apparitions began, have seen that, throughout the day and night, people are within the church praying. Most of the throngs, however, come for the evening Mass, which begins at six o'clock. (Many, however, come to the church at five o'clock – and even earlier – to say their prayers.) A number of priests are always on hand depending on the significance of a particular day and the number of pilgrims. Before and during Mass, most of the priests hear confessions. So patent is the reverence of the pilgrims that one of them said to me: "All these confessions must be doing great damage to the devil's kingdom."

The Rosary

Evening services begin with recitation of the rosary, which is normally led by one of the priests. This is always a special time: the people seem to be of one heart and one voice, in an atmosphere of God's presence. Attendance in the church every evening is always inspiring. The church has pews for only 600 people (I have never seen an empty pew), but sometimes as many as 20,000 have attended the evening service.

The Apparition

When I see the visionaries and the petitioners in the time of apparition, I believe that they represent the entire world – every individual – gathering all the world's pain and suffering and presenting it to Our Lady. Unfortunately, however, the world is unwilling to make submission to Our Lady, though it is the fervent wish of the children and their petitioner-attendants.

The room in which the Virgin appears to the children is very small, only 17 by 15 feet. The small size and the location remove all possibility of "show business." After the group enters the room, the petitioners deposit rosaries, medals, and other religious articles over which Our Lady prays a blessing. The children stand in front of the table.

Because prayer is the way we communicate with God and Our Lady, this session begins with prayer – and the prayers recommended by Our Lady: seven Our Fathers, seven Hail Marys, and seven Glorias. The children begin these prayers before there is any sign that the Virgin will appear; then, usually as they begin the second or third Our Father, they fall to their knees. (Someone has compared or likened their dropping to their knees to electrocution.) This happens at the instant Our Lady appears. The children's faces turn together as their eyes converge on one spot, about 8 feet away from them, near a crucifix.

Immediately before Our Lady appears – according to the children's testimony – they see a light, from which she emerges. The children say that all contact with and awareness of the material world is suspended during their visions. (This seems to have been borne out, as their behavior has been closely observed during times of visions. They seem totally unaware of glaring television lights and cameras, in front of them and on all sides, during the visions.) Those who are present at the visions cannot hear what is spoken between Our Lady and the children, although they see the children's lips move as they speak. They also see the children's eyes, which are bright and joyous, even if previously they'd been sad or suffering from some illness.

According to their testimony, the children pray with Our Lady. They also listen to her as she talks to them, ask her questions, and sing with her. She, in turn, talks to them, answering their questions and giving them advice. The children say that her feelings and speech are always reflected by her facial expressions. After a vision begins, the children say, the Virgin leads them in prayer. Then, with Mary as their leader, they pray the Gloria.

At times, the silence is complete; and only the children's lip movements can be seen as they speak with Our Lady. Sometimes the silence ends with a low exclamation of one (or more) of the children: "She has gone away!" The children have testified that sometimes they see a cross or a heart, and they relay this information: "There is a cross!" "There is a heart!"

Immediately after the visions, the children write out the messages or answers they have received from Our Lady, for themselves and for petitioners. If there is something special to say, they converse with the people, especially with the sick and ill. The visions usually last from 2 to 15 minutes, though some have lasted 45 minutes.

P.S. This was a description of the visionaries in 1982. Now the apparitions take place in private houses of the seers.

Number of Apparitions

Since the first apparition (June 24, 1981), with very few exceptions, Our Lady has appeared to the children every day. To some, this constitutes a difficulty. For example, a bishop asked me: "Is it possible that Our Lady would appear every day, for such a long time? This has never happened before." Perhaps the proper answer is that the mentality of the times is different from ever before. The modern mentality seems to demand a new event every day; events of even yesterday seem to have no meaning today, and indeed are immediately forgotten.

The fact is, however – as events at Međugorje prove – miracles still happen. Mary knows us and our times well, and how our minds work, and therefore appears day after day. As Fr. Janko Bubalo said to me: "I'm sure she would have been forgotten by now if she appeared in Međugorje only as often as she appeared at Fatima." When the children were told to ask Our Lady "How long will you appear to us?" she responded: "Have I begun to bore you so soon?" When, on the sixth day, the children asked: "Dear Our Lady! How many days will you stay with us?" she answered: "As long as you wish."

Evening Mass

Because of the large crowds that assembled on the hill-side every afternoon to pray and await Our Lady, the "meeting place" soon had to be transferred to the parish church – and its altar. Earlier, Our Lady had asked that Mass be celebrated every day at the approximate time of her apparition. However, the pastor came under pressure to discontinue this Mass, and he asked the children to consult Our Lady. Our Lady answered: "Continue to celebrate the Mass."

The children have no special role in this Mass, which begins at six in the evening. Sometimes Jakov serves at the altar, as do the other children, but usually they follow the Mass from the room in which the visions occur, singing with the choir and the congregation.

On December 19, 1981, the Most Rev. Frane Franić, archbishop of Split, visited Međugorje incognito and afterward wrote this report in the official newspaper of his archdiocese:

It was dark when I entered the church, which was full of people, and outside the church were cars with license plates from many cities – from Dubrovnik and Mostar, from Sarajevo to Split. There were vast crowds of people, many of whom were young. A Franciscan priest, who served the Mass, also gave the homily about faith as trust. He spoke about miracles and their meaning. It was obvious that he believes in miracles; therefore he is not tainted by some ultramodern theology or impossible exegesis. It was also obvious that he inclines to belief in the reported happenings at Međugorje – probably, in a personal sense, believes in them. At any rate, the people listened to him very attentively, including the numerous young people, who either stood or knelt.

Everything in the liturgy was according to the new Latin rite. Word for word, the celebrant read the Eucharist prayer from the missal – except that, instead of "reigns," he said "rules," in "who lives and reigns forever." There are similar changes or differences as well, but nothing important or substantial. Holy Communion is distributed throughout the church by Franciscans, in their habits and stoles, and I received the Host from one of them. Nobody recognized me, as a priest or otherwise; besides, my roman collar was concealed by a scarf. I returned to Split after the Mass and the prayer service, deeply gratified.

The archbishop's impression about prayer life in the parish was very positive, but final judgment on the authenticity of the apparitions must be left to the experts and, finally, the Church.

Probably the most popular and frequently sung hymn is the one that was specially composed by a local priest, Fr. Stanko Vasilj, in honor of the "Our Lady of Međugorje." Its melodic simplicity and expression of love for the Virgin Mary make its singing a very special moment. In Međugorje, the community's singing is much like its praying: alive and spirited.

After the Mass and a closing hymn, the pilgrims are led in prayer by the priests. They pray the seven Our Fathers, Hail Marys, Glorias, and the Credo. After this, one of the local priests relates all information pertaining to the apparitions, to the schedule in the church, especially if there has been a new development. This information is especially directed to pilgrims who have come to Međugorje for the first time.

Prayer for the Sick

The evening service ends with a prayer for the sick rosary or adoration. Many pilgrims are always on hand – some have come from the most distant places – to ask the Mother of God to intercede for them in their illnesses, asking God to heal or comfort them. Indeed, many have been healed on these occasions.

The Visionaries

Is there a difference between the year 1981, when the visions began in Međugorje and the year 1983, when this book was first published and this time. As far as the visionaries are concerned, both could be said: YES and NO.

Years have gone by; the same people are called visionaries and they say the same about what happened in the evening around 6.00 o'clock on that day June 24, 1981 on the mountain of Podbrdo and what continues afterwards. They firmly stand by their first report of having seen Our Lady. Ever since the first day, the visionaries are equally confident in that simple initial testimony. In this there is no change whatsoever.

However the life of the visionaries and the world around them did change much. All are married and live an ordinary family life. Soon after the fall of communism, a tragic war took place in Croatia and Bosnia-Herzegovina. Croatian people established their own state for the first time since they lost it in the 11th century. In the meantime, the Catholics of Bosnia-Herzegovina experienced the most tragic exodus in their history and their number was reduced to half (from 900,000 to 450,000).

Observing the visionaries, one may notice their three permanent qualities:

1) A decisive commitment to work and witness for Our Lady. Their commitment is not hindered by fear of public opinion, pressures, expectations or any other imposed human condition.

2) In their relaxed and confident way, the visionaries keep their freedom intact. One of their friends observed them as willing and able to make decisions contrary to the expectations of pilgrims, priests of the parish or people of the village.

3) The mentality of the visionaries during these years of special spiritual calling has been kept rooted into the local mentality of their own people. People are impressed as to how normal and human they are. While Our Lady calls Her children, She keeps their free will miraculously intact and lets everyone walk on their own ordinary human way.

How Do the Visionaries See Our Lady?

The visionaries say they see Our Lady the same way we see people in regular life, that is, in three dimensions. First they see a bright light, from which Our Lady emerges. However, when they are "immersed" in the vision, they do not see and have no awareness of anything else. They do not react to anything else around them – people moving about, taking photographs, or simply staring.

The visions last two to 45 minutes, but usually between 5 and 10 minutes. At the end, Our Lady disappears in the light from which she emerged. Sometimes, before the light disappears, they see images or symbols: the sun, a cross, a heart. When Fr. Tomislav asked Vicka to explain these images, she said: "She (Our Lady) said the cross is the sign of salvation, the sun shines on us from above, and the heart is the sign of her Son's love." In other words, the sun is life; it shines and vivifies us. The cross is salvation. The heart is the love of Jesus Christ.

The children say they do not have the words to describe the beauty of Our Lady. Her face is human but her beauty is divine. The color of her body and the harmony between her figure and her clothing cannot be described or compared with anything we have seen. One of the children said: "I could look at her – and look and look forever!" Her voice, they say, is very pleasant, like beautiful music, and she speaks in perfect Croatian.

During the visions, as we have noted, no one can hear the children speak; all that can be perceived is the movement of their lips and facial expressions. (Agreement on this observation is unanimous.) Nevertheless, all the facial expressions are similar, and the observer is convinced that, whatever the children perceive, it is unique to them: the knowledge, emotions, and the experience itself. Their expressions and rapt attention indicate the intensity of the experience.

Content of the Messages

Seeing Our Lady is, in itself, a message, a gift; it imprints a permanent mark on a person. Hearing her words, receiving her messages, is like hearing God himself and receiving his message. However, the messages do not convey any new teachings. We have heard nothing we had not already heard over and over in the past, before the first apparition. Jesus has already told us everything, the final word, and we can read it all in the Bible. But still, in a sense, it is new, because it comes to us in a new way and touches the modern world. With Mother it is always like that. Her love never changes and it is always old and always new.

Our Lady does not present herself as a savior, but comes as a servant and messenger of the Savior, exuding a special kind of motherly love. Because the messages she brings come from God, they reaffirm the conditions for our salvation and the salvation of the world. They restate the conditions for peace in the world for the very existence of the world.

The messages are simple: peace, conversion, faith, prayer, and penance and fasting. These messages are meant for the entire world, and the six visionaries have been given a special responsibility to convey them. (The children, variously, have received personal messages, which do not have a universal dimension.)

When I asked the children to ask Our Lady if she has a special message for me, if God has a special plan for me, because of a special situation in which I found myself, they answered: "Pray more and do more penance!" and "Wherever God calls you, go!"

In this part of Bosnia and Herzegovina, in the diocese of Mostar, the "Case of Herzegovina" has been common knowledge for several years. When the children were asked to consult Our Lady about this, they answered: "Prayer and patience are required." And if anyone asks them what prayers people should say, for various reasons, their answer is always to pray the old, recommended prayers and to fast and do penance. If some are unable to fast, others can fast on their behalf.

The answers that the children bring from Our Lady are always wise, dignified, and respectful of every person and his freedom, as well as tactful and, somehow, reminiscent of maternal love and caring. Their content and meaning transcends the ability of children to fabricate.

The Secrets

In addition to the recommendations (above), the children claim that Our Lady said she would impart secrets to them and them alone. Some of these secrets have to do with the world, some with the local church and parish, and some with the Church as a whole. Other secrets are private or personal, only for the six children.

Three of the secrets are known by all of the children, and will be revealed only after Our Lady instructs them to do so. Their fidelity is first to Our Lady, so that the influence of those they respect – the local priests, the bishop, their parents – is unavailing in such matters. Indeed, the children guard their secrets with the utmost tenacity, without giving the slightest hint of their content. This, however, confirms the authority of the source of the secrets, as well as the children's love and respect for that source.

The Apparitions Described

The appearance of Our Lady is always preceded by a splendor of light, described by the children as "glowing with holiness." When she appears, Our Lady wears a white veil, and her gown is not bound at her waist but flows straight down and conceals her feet. Her dress is a bright, luminous gray, which the children find hard to describe. A small black curl is seen on the left side of her face.

On only one occasion was Mary dressed differently: on August 15, the Feast of the Assumption. After this apparition, all the children said she was exceptionally beautiful and "dressed all in gold!"

Our Lady's complexion is like that of country girls of the region: olive in hue with reddish cheeks. Her facial expression varies, according to stimuli, as do the expressions of people in everyday life. Her expressions range from joy and happiness to sadness and grief. Her hands are raised in an attitude "typical of charismatic prayer."

On certain feast days, such as Christmas, she appears with the Baby Jesus in her arms. On major feast days, she is smiling and joyous; she wears the same clothing, but it is more brilliant in appearance. "You could never find anything like it on earth!" These feast days are St. James (July 25), the Assumption (Aug. 15), the Nativity of Mary (Sept. 8), the Exaltation of the Cross (second Sunday of September), the Immaculate Conception (Dec. 8), Christmas and Easter, and June 24 – the anniversary of the day she first appeared to the children and June 25, the day she wishes to see designated the Feast of Our Lady, Queen of Peace.

Heaven, Hell, Purgatory

All six children have told us that Our Lady has shown them Heaven, and invited them to see Hell (which two of them asked not to see because of their great fear). Our Lady, explaining why she was doing this, said: "I am showing you Heaven and Hell so that you can see for yourself what reward God has prepared for those who love him and what punishment awaits those who offend him!"

Vicka and Jakov, moreover, say that they were actually taken to Heaven, that they disappeared from earth for twenty minutes. During those twenty minutes, it is known, Jakov's mother searched for him, because she had seen him in the house shortly before he disappeared. Fearing that something might have happened, she looked for him diligently, inside and outside the house, but Vicka and Jakov could not be found. The moment they returned, Jakov told his mother what had happened and where they had been; and both of them told her they had seen Heaven and Hell, and had passed through Purgatory. They described Heaven as a region of great light and happiness; Hell as a sea of fire, with blackened figures moving about; and Purgatory as a great darkness, in which everyone's face was vague and dim.

The Great Sign

One of the secrets that the children speak about is the "great sign" Our Lady will leave at the site of her first appearance – a sign or testimony for those who do not believe. Many miraculous healings will be performed with it. The children know what the sign will be, and four of them know the date, but they give no further information about it because the rest is part of the secret. "I know that many will not believe you", the Virgin told the children, "and many who are enthusiastic for the faith will grow cold; but you stay steadfast and urge all people to prayer, penance, and conversion. At the end, you will be the happiest."

Unusual Events

As we have indicated, the children are not the only ones who have witnessed miraculous happenings. Besides those who have been healed, many people, especially from Bijakovići, have seen a number of very unusual events. On August 2, 1981 (the Feast of Our Lady Queen of Angels), in late afternoon, before the sun had set, the sun was seen to spin in its orbit, then descend toward the watching people (approximately 150), then retreat – a "dance of the sun" that reminded the people of the miraculous phenomenon at Fatima. When the people were able to look at the sun without hurting their eyes, they saw figures around the sun, as it seemed to circle, in the shape of a cross. The strange phenomena caused many to cry, or pray, or even run away. Then six small hearts appeared in the sky, centered around a large heart. Then a white cloud covered the hill and the site of the first apparition, and the sun returned to its normal place. The people interpreted this unusual happening as the sun's witnessing to its creator. All of this happened over approximately fifteen minutes. Priests in Međugorje urge the pilgrims never to look into the sun. The miracle of the sun is not common and often and it does not have to perform for curious people. Watching it may seriously damage the eyes.

The Cross

Some witness about the pillar of light. This is at the place of the cross. This cross was erected or built by the parishioners of Međugorje in 1933 in honor of Our Lord Jesus Christ and the nineteen-hundredth anniversary of his death. The name of the hill (Šipovac) was changed to Križevac, because in Croatian *križ* means cross. Old people, who had lived in that vicinity all their lives, said they had never seen anything like this before. Moreover, they believed it was their cross that they had seen in the sky! They only explanation, of course, is that this was a miraculous sign, given by God.

Others claim that, rather than a cross, they saw the bright figure of a woman. They claim that this has happened on several occasions, at various times of day, and on clear and cloudy days alike, and that it lasts from a few minutes to half an hour.

A Fire of Unknown Cause

On October 28, 1981, a fire of unknown origin erupted on the site of the first apparition and burned for about fifteen minutes. Several hundred people saw this, including many priests and nuns. A guard, who had been stationed at the foot of the hill to prevent pilgrims from climbing to the top, later investigated the site but found no remains of the fire. Indeed, the fire had burned brightly, but consumed nothing.

The visionaries did not see the fire because all were home at that time; in the evening vision, however, Our Lady asked if they had seen the fire, and when they said they had not, she said: "This is one of the heralds of the great sign." The children testify that the Virgin Mary has told them there will be many more such signs throughout the world, in Međugorje and other parts of the world, before the "great sign."

Soon after Our Lady made her first request for peace, a bright inscription of the word peace (*mir* in Croatian) appeared in the sky over the hill called Križevac. This was at night, early in July. The inscription was seen by the pastor and several people from the village, and they have testified to this in writing. Others have also testified to seeing the cross, which they describe as forming a T (i.e., a tau cross): "It (the crossbar) turned gray while the vertical part remained white."

Since June 24 of 1981 to Christmas of 1982, according to the testimony of the six children, Our Lady has appeared to them every day. Since Christmas of 1982, however, she has not appeared to Mirjana Dragičević, but only to the other five. Similarly, there was a seven-day period when Our Lady did not appear to Ivan Dragičević, at the time he began studies at the seminary in Dubrovnik. Our Lady told him this cessation would be temporary, until he became accustomed to the new way of life at the seminary. Finally, to test their faith – according to Vicka's testimony – there were five days in which the Virgin did not appear to the children.

Reflections

Since the first vision, many million people have visited Međugorje, most of them as pilgrims but some through simple curiosity. There have been many claims of miraculous healings, conversions, deep experiences of fervent prayer and profound insight, and the sense or conviction of God's presence. At the same time, there have been furious attacks and slanderous statements by people and by institutions. In fact, the pastor was arrested and jailed. In short, there was great joy and blessedness among many, and enmity, fear, and curses and blasphemy from some.

X

THE VISIONARIES

For more than twenty months, the six children of Međugorje have believed, and proclaimed, that they see Our Lady. Although the day-to-day lives of the people in the region do not militate against things spiritual, the social and political mores of the time certainly do not encourage spirituality. If anything, they militate against it.

Jakov, the youngest of the six visionaries, was 11 years old at the time of the first vision. Now with his family he lives at Bijakovići. Vicka, the oldest, was 17 when the apparitions began. She was the last to get married and now lives at Krehin Gradac, the parish of Gradina. Mirjana is married and lives at Bijakovići. Ivanka is married and lives at Miletina. Marija lives in Italy but with her family often stays at their home in Bijakovići. Ivan, his wife and children live in the USA. In the summertime and for major feast days they stay at their home in Međugorje.

While at school their performance ranged from average to below average. Having said this, we must also say that we do not intend to disparage the six children. Indeed, Our Lady does not belittle them; and we must remind ourselves of the words of St. Paul: "God chose those whom the world considers absurd to shame the wise; he singled out the weak of this world to shame the strong." Moreover, Our Lady told the children: "I did not look for those who are the best."

Bijakovići, the village where all the visionaries were born, is in every way virtually identical with all other villages in that part of B&H. To this time, there has been no hint – much less allegation – that there has been a plot or conspiracy either to initiate or exploit a "cult of the six visionaries." The people of the area are simple, pious, hardworking people who are utterly incapable of fraud.

None of the six children was known personally by any of the area priests prior to the revelation of June 1981. Fr. Jozo arrived in Međugorje November 11, 1980, and Fr. Zrinko arrived less than two months before him. Later in a letter, Fr. Zrinko wrote to me:

> When I arrived at the (Međugorje) rectory, late in the evening of June 26, 1981, four priests were waiting for me. One of them was the bishop's secretary. They asked me to take them to the visionaries, but I did not know the children, nor their parents or families. Unfortunately, it had not occurred to me to question the messenger who, the night before, had brought me the news about the people who now claimed to have seen Our Lady or where they had seen her.

No one in the village, priest or lay person, knew of any special religious inclination among the six children – of anything at all that would differentiate any of them from anyone else in the village. An expert in mystical theology and psychology told me:

> If I could choose a group to work with, I would not choose this one; they're too disparate in age and temperament. The youngest is 11 and the oldest is

18, and the two "leaders" (Vicka and Mirjana) are so individualistic that it would be almost impossible to produce what we have seen here. Individually and as a group, their certainty in the apparitions cannot be shaken or weakened.

When Fr. Tomislav queried Vicka about a detail of one of the messages, he asked her: "Are you sure?" and Vicka responded, simply and tersely: "How could we not be sure? We were there."

Yugoslavia's form of government is socialist-communist, and though there is freedom of religion, it must be practiced privately. Religion, nonetheless, is an important part of everybody's life, but it cannot be taught in the schools. In short, their religion was a distinct disadvantage to these children, politics being what it is. The children had nothing whatever to gain by deliberately engaging in any activity that is repressed by the government and its institutions.

Nevertheless, the children did not solicit "older and wiser heads" for advice on relating their messages from Our Lady. Everything was conducted naturally, as a matter of course, without fear of consequences for their words and actions. They did what they thought they had to do, in the manner of children. A statement by one of the children at the time of the first apparition is significant: "The only ones who do not believe us are the priests and the people from the government." Thus, unaware of the consequences, in their childlike way they have bypassed all authorities, those of the Church and those the state, because their messages come from a greater authority.

A legitimate question: Are the children "sick"? Have they received any kind of treatment, before and/or after the apparitions? It is a medical fact that many illnesses can cause hallucinations or "visions." Also, autosuggestion is a possibility. Can the phenomena associated with the children be caused by parapsychological powers? These questions must be answered in our search for the truth.

On Saturday, June 27 (as we said), the children were taken to the nearby police station and, after long and thorough examination by the police, were sent to the local medical clinic, where they were examined by Dr. Ante Vujević. Because of political tension and pressure from the police, there was not mutual trust between the doctor, who was in a difficult situation, and the children, who saw him as another prosecutor. Ivan Dragičević and Vicka Ivanković were examined by the doctor until 6:00 p.m., at which time the children ran from the clinic to the hillside to keep their appointment with Our Lady. Dr. Ante, a general practitioner, made this statement: "These children seem to be perfectly healthy, but it is not within my competence to make the final judgment."

Parapsychological Influence?

"Parapsychological" can mean something good or bad, a healthy or unhealthy condition; so if one says the children may be under some parapsychological influence, this is not necessarily bad or evil. Simply put, "parapsychological influence" cannot be explained in entirety as "psychological influence" alone; that is, it goes beyond the boundaries of psychology. We do not know all the psychological and parapsychological forces that may be operant in humans – nor, of course, their limits. Despite all advances in our understanding of what humans are and what "makes them tick," many areas are shrouded in mystery. For Christians, revelation is our only knowledge and guide through such areas.

Nevertheless, fear has been voiced that, somehow, the children's "parapsychology" has been manipulated – has been used or misused. Such voices have been raised despite the total absence of indications and proof, merely on the basis of guesses, speculation, or sheer possibility. The question, in short, is whether the children have become victims of human manipulation, to which experts (such as Dr. Stopar) say no. To be manipulated, a medium must first be subjected to lengthy preparation, then led or coached in short bursts of performance over a very limited time. All this, the experts say, is easy to detect; and to transform such a diverse group of humans into uniform automatons is impossible. There is simply no basis for such allegations in Međugorje.

Diabolical Influence?

The effects of the devil's influence are well known: destruction of the personalities he influences and works through. Such people are full of conflicts and anxiety and moreover, in their vanity and egotism, proud of it. Their attitudes are negative, and they lead others in that direction. The influence of the devil is often at the root of unhealthy psychological impulses.

One day, after Mass in Međugorje, I heard a comment that reduced all this to common sense: "If the devil has anything to do with this, he's made the mistake of his life." As Scripture says: "You will recognize them by their fruits" (Mt 7:16), and hundreds of thousands have recognized God's work in the children. A cardinal of the Church said to me: "I feel that the devil is uneasy about this; so there must be something good in all this." He meant in Međugorje.

Influence of Parish Priests?

Parish priests, as well as the nuns and the overall religious atmosphere, may have had an undue influence upon the phenomena at Međugorje. Indeed, critics who wish him ill refer to the pastor, Fr. Jozo Zovko, as creator of a *"*Međugorje conspiracy."

At the time of the first vision, Fr. Zovko was the newly appointed pastor and, as such, was unacquainted with his parishioners. Moreover, on the evening of June 24, 1981, he was 400 kilometers away, at a meeting at a seminary in Zagreb. By the time he returned to Međugorje, news of the apparition had spread far and wide, and Fr. Zovko was powerless to suppress it. Accordingly, he decided to dampen, if not disparage, the effect of the reports by referring to "stories" of apparitions that "might be just a religious and pastoral diversion." In any event, his emphasis was on his habitual preaching of the Gospel and celebration of the Eucharist, together with urging the people to pray and continue to practice their traditional religious duties. He dissuaded his parishioners from putting credence in the "stories" of the six children.

Approximately seven days after the first apparition, however, Fr. Jozo changed his stand; he became a supporter – indeed a preacher – of the truthfulness of the apparitions. Now his emphasis fell on the connection between the Church's traditional teaching and the messages from Our Lady.

The story of Fr. Zrinko Čuvalo is distinctly different. Even now, the children remember him with fear. Instead of sympathy or tolerance, they received from him rejection and disbelief. A "realist of the old school," he was uncomfortable with the changes in the Church and was bureaucratic and rigid in his approach to things. When people tried to approach him to talk about the visions, he would retreat to his garden to do something "worthwhile" and not "waste my time." His role, in short, was that of a Doubting Thomas, and it goes without saying that no one ever accused him of conspiring to "fake" the visions. In fact, those who shared his thinking hoped he "would put an end to all this nonsense."

Later, however, when Fr. Jozo was put in jail and Fr. Zrinko became pastor in his place, the latter did not try to end the "nonsense." He converted to belief in the visions. Through all ensuing difficult and trying times, he stood firmly on the side of the children and those who believed in the visions. Then, exhausted by tension and additional work, he asked that either more priests be sent to help at Međugorje or that he be replaced. He has been reassigned to another parish, but now, whenever he visits Međugorje, he comes as a pious pilgrim and is received as a very dear guest.

The two priests who were assigned to Međugorje at the time of the first visions have been reassigned, and had no influence on the initial phenomenon or later developments. The children and the stream of pilgrims account for all developments, though, each in his way, Frs. Zovko and Čuvalo were part of a process that exalts God. The priests who replaced Frs. Zovko and Čuvalo cannot be related to the early apparitions in any way. Fr. Tomislav Pervan, the pastor, and Fr. Tomislav Vlašić, the associate pastor, were assigned in Ljubuški and Čapljina, and had never before been assigned to Međugorje. The new pastor was assigned to Međugorje almost one year after the apparitions began, and Fr. Vlašić just a little before that.

Influence of Sisters?

At the time of the first apparitions, two nuns were stationed in Međugorje: Sr. Vladimira Vučić and Sr. Marcelina Sušac (both of whom were about to be reassigned to different parishes). Because of their short stay in Međugorje, their stand in opposition to reports of the visions, and the nature of their parish work, no one has even suggested that they might have helped falsify the visions. (No other persons, in any capacity, can be connected with the origin of the visions or with the visionaries.)

The Visionaries

Now we must examine the possibility that the children, individually and/or as a group, initiated the visions.

At that time, Vida (Vicka) Ivanković was 17 (born Sept. 3, 1964). Her father was a migrant worker in West Germany. Vicka, with her very strong will, is the natural leader of the group; she is full of energy, courageous and outspoken in dealing with people and situations, and has a well-developed sense of responsibility. When Our Lady said that it was not good for all children to leave Međugorje to continue their high school studies in nearby Mostar (leaving little Jakov behind by himself), Vicka immediately volunteered to drop out of school to tend to Jakov.

The rough appearance of her hands, covered with scratches, indicates that she works regularly in the fields. She dresses so simply that it is obvious she has no great thought for her appearance. During the visions, however, hers is the most interesting face to study.

Our question, then, is whether Vicka initiated the group and the alleged apparitions. According to the testimony of the other members of the group, she ran away from the "strange and dangerous" site of the first vision. Neither Vicka nor anyone else, however, has ever maintained, or indicated, that she – or any of them – is a "center" or initiator. The center of all their interest and devotion is Our Lady, whom they claim to see.

Mirjana (Miriam) Dragičević (born Mar. 18, 1965) was 16 at the time of the first vision. Mirjana is a "modern person" – that is, similar to those we see every day on the streets of our cities. The brightest and best educated of the group, she has given the clearest and most descriptive accounts of the apparitions and messages. Also, she is the first one to have ceased to have these visions. Neither before nor after this cessation did she play a special role in the group. Even before she ceased to have visions, she was seldom with the group. She is very strong in her faith in God and in asserting the truthfulness of the visions. She says that Our Lady promised to appear to her every year on her birthday. In Our Lady's appearance for her birthdays, Mirjana says, most of the time she encourages her in faith.

There have been allegations that Mirjana initiated the group, but I have found no evidence for this.

Ivan (John) Dragičević was 16 in 1981. He was born May 25, 1965. Like most children, Ivan needed a push to say his prayers and go to church. But four days after the first apparition, his mother said: "Yesterday, for the first time since he was born, I found a rosary in a pocket of his pants." Almost immediately, she noticed a profound change in him. He was known as extremely shy. In school his abilities were not outstanding, and those who know him best cannot imagine that he would be willing or able to initiate the events in Međugorje. Often he speaks at many churches and Marian conferences all over the world.

Marija Pavlović – Lunetti (born Apr. 1, 1965), is the most serene and deeply spiritual of the visionaries. People are impressed by her pious personality; they see her as a beautiful and obedient servant of God and Our Lady. All who know her describe her as "just beautiful" because of her deep spirituality, prayerfulness, and humility. When Our Lady called upon her to pray more, she always responded, thus forming a deeper commitment to prayer and spiritual growth.

People approach the visionaries with deep respect, sometimes even fear, because they sense something in them that is unusually spiritual, almost divine. Marija, however, is gifted in making people feel comfortable in her presence. She has a good word for everybody. There are no indications that Marija formed or helped form the group. For one thing, she is not a take-charge type of person. She appears to be the type of person who listens attentively, then acts upon the instructions or wishes of those she listens.

Ivica (Ivanka) Ivanković – Elez, (born June 21, 1966), seems to be more superficial, and thus typical of a modern person, than the others in the group. At the same time, she is level headed and not impetuous in action and statements. Ivanka also has forgone going further in school. Although she was the person who first saw Our Lady, she has no special status in the group.

Many people have tried to extract the "secrets" from the children, and once, while talking to Ivanka, I learned first hand how careful and diligent they are in maintaining them. If someone asks them to speak about the secrets, they refuse to talk or continue what they have been doing.

Ivanka, like all the other visionaries, is very independent of the group, which functions equally well with or without a particular member. None of the visionaries thinks the existence or function of the group depends in any way upon his or her presence. She lives very private life in Miletina. Ivanka, Mirjana and since Sep. 12. 1998. Jakov do not have apparitions every day.

Jakov (James) Čolo was born March 6, 1971. Jakov's intelligence and firmness of faith are unusual and demand respect. When asked by a priest to write the secrets on a piece of paper and leave them with the priest, Jakov said: "I could, as well, write the secrets out and keep them with me at home." Fr. Tomislav Pervan once described Jakov as "too young for deep spirituality, but his role in the apparitions is a strong argument for their authenticity." His further explanation was like this: "Any normal child, such as Jakov, would soon rebel against going somewhere every day – for years – simply to make a show that he was seeing something miraculous, whether on a hillside or in a church. When someone expressed concern about Jakov's ability to keep the secrets, Vicka spoke up: "He is the strongest!" Jakov, certainly, has proven himself to be sufficiently strong. In those years at the beginning the uninformed observer would see him only as a typical 12-year-old boy. For me this caused me to reflect that every young boy and girl, and every person of whatever age, is a special being to God and to Our Lady.

While on his journey in America Jakov reported the following text to us from Miami.

"On Friday September 11th 1998, during the regular apparition Our Lady told me to prepare myself specially by prayer for tomorrow's apparition because she will confide the 10th secret to me. On Saturday September 12th Our Lady came at 11:15 (local time). When she came she greeted me as always with 'Praised be Jesus'. While she was confiding the 10th secret to me she was sad.

Then with a gentle smile she said to me: 'Dear child! I am your mother and I love you unconditionally. From today I will not be appearing to you every day, but only on Christmas, the birthday of my Son. Do not be sad, because as a mother I will always be with you and like every true mother I will never leave you. And you continue further to follow the way of my Son, the way of peace and love and try to persevere in the mission that I have confided to you. Be an example of that man who has known God and God's love. Let people always see in you an example of how God acts on people and how God acts through them. I bless you with my motherly blessing and I thank you for having responded to my call'. The apparition ended at 11:45."

Gifts, Mission, Responsibilities

We, at our human, earthly level, see the six children as an instrument or cause of all that happens in Međugorje – all that is avowedly supernatural. The children, nevertheless, remain what they are: young people. All who have seen them and talked with them are most impressed that they seem so normal, so childlike, so similar to everyone else their age. They have not become affected or overbearing, or "saintly." Our Lady has not, so to speak, commandeered their youth, but consents to their full range of freedom. Her coming to see them is a gift they have received from God and Our Lady, and they have been invited to receive the gift and share it with others. Their faith in what they have seen, the messages, and the visions themselves are gifts, special graces, from God. Though they are still adolescents, or at most young adults, they seem to feel very comfortable, fully at ease, unembarrassed, and completely without fear.

The children, as is evident, have received special graces, but immense responsibilities as well that they seem not to be aware of. Our Lady has told them they will have to suffer "witnessing" for receiving her messages. And ever since the first apparition, the children, very obediently, attend a long liturgical service every evening with no complaints but, rather, with joy and love and a mature responsibility. For children like them, this is tantamount to suffering, a consequence of their calling.

Believers who come to Međugorje see the experience as a form of communion between the divine and the human. The children, the pilgrims to Međugorje, and the people who live there are very human, just as the rocks and soil and hills are earthy; and on the other side of the equation is God, manifesting his will to man. An expert on mystical theology said to me: "The children's experience is clearly transcendence, a direct involvement with God. This cannot be a result of human effort, of human prayer, alone."

Why Does the Group Endure?

On the human, pragmatic level, nothing could make this group cohere for any great length of time. Its members have no mutual, personal interest in the group as such, neither in its formation nor its persistence. At the same time, many elements and circumstances could be said to have worked against its formation and persistence. The only plausible explanation for all this is the one the children assert: Our Lady wills it. Freely, the children are willing to live and die, to sacrifice, to be rejected or even condemned for what they claim is the truth. They do not know how long their group will last, except, they say, "As long as Our Lady wants it to last." Obviously, the authority behind their visions takes priority over every other authority in their lives, and keeps the group together.

These children have no wish for money or fine clothing. Likewise they disdain food and drink. Rather, day by day they give witness to what they preach, and fast on bread and water two days in every week. They do not accept money from people who offer it to them. They expect no reward for what they do. If thankful pilgrims succeed in forcing money on them, they give the money to the parish. Although Fr. Tomislav has offered to give them what money they might require from time to time, none of them has made such a request.

Their words are so convincing and their example so powerful that their neighbors in the village and thousands upon thousands of pilgrims (including many priests and nuns) listen closely to what they say and follow their example. Disagreements have arisen among the visionaries, but none pertaining to the apparitions or the messages.

After more than two years, they show no sign of discouragement. There have been threats of physical harm to them and their families, their private lives have all but disappeared, and the village has suffered very unpleasant moments and experiences (e.g., the pastor was arrested and thrown in jail). But nothing has discouraged them. There is not the merest hint that they ever considered "backing off." Instead, the greater the difficulties, the firmer their resolve.

In short, the reason for the group – its formation and continued existence – surpasses human reason. Still, the children tell us the reason: Our Lady wills it.

Our Lady and the Children

The love that Our Lady seems to radiate to the children is the only possible explanation of the children's response.

This, in turn, is reflected in the children's love, fidelity, and honor of Our Lady.

The children's freedom is perfectly intact. There is no sign of enslavement, of blind obedience, in their relationship with Our Lady. However, it seems she has conquered their hearts in a caring, loving, motherly way. Tactfully, one might say, she leads them by suggestion: delivering messages, sharing secrets, advising them in personal matters. In turn, they readily listen to everything she says, tell her their concerns, ask questions, and sing and pray with her. In unique, loving freedom, the children have chosen Our Lady somewhat as she has chosen them. The words of Our Lady seem to grow and develop within them, to affect their lives, and though they serve her obediently, they relate her messages without fear.

The first time I entered the "vision room," I was filled with apprehension, but the children were smiling and comfortable and perfectly at ease. Despite their great respect for Our Lady, they harbor not the least bit of fear of her. Moreover, her motherly affection and protection have been put to the test several times, when the children have been threatened by pressures from Church and state alike. Every time, they have firmly stood their ground.

Our Lady is a tremendous teacher. Her attention is individually bestowed, so that each child feels unique and individual in being specially loved. All who know them think of them as six individuals, disparate in background and temperament, who – somehow, for whatever reason – were called to form a group of visionaries.

Whenever Our Lady imparts a word of correction to one of them, he or she (and no one else) hears it. Otherwise, when they are together, they see, hear, and react the same way, as if in unison. Our Lady's corrections are gently delivered, but are not to be ignored.

The relationship between Our Lady and the children is deep and profound, but not indulgent or self-centered. Today, the attention paid to the needs of others – parents, friends, priests – is greater than ever before. The admission (and experience) of the parish priests is that they require the help of others to grow in personal maturity and spirituality.

This is the way of life in the Church: God is present and at work in the lives of his people, but he wants them to cooperate with him on their salvation and the salvation of the world. In the words of Our Lady, as reported by the children: "Whenever you have difficulties and need help, come to me."

XI

OUR LADY'S PURPOSE

We are very limited in our ways of thinking: by our age, habits, mentality; and we do not see other possibilities. Therefore, when something new, unusual, surprising occurs, we seem almost dumbfounded and ask why. Why Our Lady? Why now? Why there? Why to these children?

One way of trying to stay in touch with the world is through television, newspapers, books, and many other sources of information. Being in touch through these sources, we tend to believe we are in touch with everything. When, on television, we see a person dying of hunger, we think we are in touch with what is happening – in touch with that person. But such is not the case. We have lost touch with that dying person and his world. In other words, we have lost meaningful touch with much of the world, with other people, other human beings.

On the movie screen we see "stars" who represent real people in real situations – but are they real, the people and the situations? "By their fruits will you know them" is the criterion we must apply. Our newspapers and magazines often pander, in their frenzy to "make money," to the basest human instincts, to the most transient and superficial "needs" of man, and thereby distort or pervert life itself. With a vengeance, the same is true of television. Indeed, the mass media do not judge success by the good they do in promoting the well-being of man, but in dollars and cents, and we know that commercial success and the well-being of man do not necessarily go hand in hand.

Even the Church, very often, seems to have reconciled herself to secular preoccupations. When she raises her lonely voice in the modern wilderness, the world chooses not to listen, as if the Church were an infant and therefore unable to tell grown-ups what to do.

Thus Our Lady has become a prophetess for our time, which has lost touch with itself and with God. Thus we learn the answer to the question "Why Our Lady?" She wants to put us in touch again. Therefore she has come to Međugorje, and thus to the world.

Obraćenje (Conversion)

"In times past, God spoke in fragmentary and varied ways to our fathers through the prophets; in this, the final age, he has spoken to us through his Son" (Heb 1:1-2). Now, in the Holy Spirit, he continues to speak to us through the Mother of his Son, the Blessed Virgin Mary.

Every time the children are asked about the "main message" of Our Lady, their answers may vary in wording but their meaning is always the same: In the words of Marija: "All the messages concern the world, such as conversion, faith, peace, prayer, and fasting and penance."

Conversion, then, is a basic message from Međugorje – and conversion is a basic message in all prophecy. Mary, as a special prophet of our time, calls and encourages all people to conversion. Earlier, Jeremiah called his people to conversion, telling them: "Cleanse your heart of evil" (Jer 4:14). Cleansing one's heart – conversion – is effected through the saving power of God, and Our Lady intends to convey the power of conversion from God to all peoples, to every person. It is not a message of fear or threat, but God's loving plan to bring each person into his kingdom.

The prophet Ezekiel, together with his people, asked: "How can we survive?" Even in Ezekiel's time, the final judgment was rendered, for he told his people: "As I live, says the Lord God, I swear I take no pleasure in the death of the wicked man, but in the wicked man's conversion, that he may live" (Ez 33:10-11).

The cause of all man's sufferings – catastrophes, tragedies, wars – is his lack of faith in God. All the alternatives that man has tried have proved unavailing; Sartre explained how far men can go when he said: "The devil is the only one who deserves respect, because he dares to stand against God." Our Lady, in opposition to Sartre and his ilk, says: Only God deserves our respect.

The uncleansed heart is the source of every evil: hate, greed, selfishness, fraud, violence, war. These evils reach into every corner of the world, into every person, every nation, every people of every race and color. The victims are not only those on whom these evils are imposed, but also those who impose them.

It is the human heart that maintains wars between nations, seeks to build Godless societies, urges enterprises of selfishness and crime, enacts inhuman laws. Thus children are burdened with the sins of their fathers, and new generations are burdened with all the sins of their ancestors. Nations are burdened with the sins and faults of other nations, and the weight of all this oppresses people to the verge of destruction. God prefers to remove all this, to lighten our burdens. God wants to renew our hearts, to fill them with his Spirit of Love, to change the whole world.

The most important negotiations for war and peace are conducted in the individual heart, and peace will come when man reconciles himself with God. Conversion, then, is the only alternative to our sinful, self-destructive course in life. "If we say we are free of the guilt of sin, we deceive ourselves; the truth is not to be found in us... We make him a liar" (1 John 1:8, 9). Because everyone is a sinner, no one is excluded from conversion.

God has died, so to speak, in the lives of many nominal Christians, who seek no union with him. Others may even attend church and perform their traditional duties, but many do it without faith. To them, as well, Our Lady says: "Convert before it is too late, while there is time!"

Although Our Lady does not speak to terrorize people, she speaks of the consequences of one's choice. When she showed the sight of Hell to the visionaries, she said: "This is the punishment of those who do not love God; and many who are alive today will go to Hell."

The means of conversion are prayer, penance, fasting, and monthly confession. In response to her call for conversion, many people have resumed praying, fasting, and various forms of penance, and long lines of penitent pilgrims receive the sacrament of reconciliation in Međugorje.

On one occasion, Our Lady expressed satisfaction when she saw that people were praying, fasting, and improving their way of living. In 1981, on the eve of the Feast of the Immaculate Conception, she said: "Many people have begun their conversion, but not all." The next day, when the children expected to see Our Lady happy and joyful because it was her feast day, they were vastly surprised: Our Lady was very serious, almost downcast. Kneeling, she opened her arms to the sky and began to pray: "My beloved Son! Please forgive those numerous, serious sins with which humanity offends you!" She continued to pray in this vein, though the children do not re-member her exact words. When she had finished this prayer, she led the children in praying Our Fathers and the Glorias. Then she told them that she prays daily at the foot of the cross, asking her Son to forgive humanity's sins. Before she left, however, she smiled on the children, not wanting to leave them in sorrow.

We can well conclude that the accumulation of sin in the world is so intense that it has brought mankind to the brink of self-destruction. It is not within the means of man to fashion a system of protection that would save him from the fate that man is preparing for himself. God, nonetheless, offers the only option: conversion.

"Glory to God in the highest, and peace on earth to those on whom his favor rests" (Lk 2:14). Peace is God's greeting to, his acknowledgment of, man. Praise of His glory is man's greeting to God.

When Mary brought her Son's message to the world, angels sang praises of his glory and "peace on earth to those on whom his favor rests." Thus Mary (together with the Church) is the permanent bearer of her Son to the world, which celebrates eternal Christmas with her. She brings her Son to every age, every country, every man and woman. Her Son is the newborn child, the ever-present God, who comes to bring peace and to reconcile Heaven and earth.

God Is Peace

Perfect peace is God and man together. Those who have God's favor, who trust in him, receive his peace.

Wars signify God's absence from humans' lives; thus war is the absence of peace. All wars begin in the human heart and despoil all families and all the world.

The absence of war is not necessarily a time of peace. In our time, and throughout history, copious tears have been shed because so many people and nations have been enslaved in times of ostensible peace. In contrast, God's peace consists in reverence for God himself and for others.

In our day and age, man has formed a mentality that tells him war is rational and unavoidable. War is said to be in keeping with man's nature and deeply rooted in him; that is, ruthless and ever aggressive.

War assumes many forms: between peoples, nations, religions, corporations, husbands and wives, and in individuals' hearts and minds. The consequences are grievous, for the devil's harvest is immense.

With this mentality, we come to believe that peace is very fragile, that it shatters very easily at the slightest jar. Moreover, we have been so suborned and misled that the concepts of war and peace have been separated from our concepts of religion and the world. In our minds, we have adapted to a constant state of war, and are almost reconciled to living with such misconceptions.

Our Lady's peace, God's peace, excludes all notions and aspects of war: injustice, fear, anxiety, and even death.

In Međugorje, Our Lady beseeches that we reach out to God. "Make yourself a new heart and a new spirit! Why should you die?" (Ez 18:31). Presenting her Son for peace and reconciliation, she invites us to celebrate a permanent Christmas. Through conversion, she offers to lead us to the house of peace.

On the third day of the apparitions, when the children asked: "Dear Our Lady! Why have you come here?" she answered: "I come to convert and reconcile people." Mary, therefore, is another incarnation of God's will. She does not offer empty promises. Her word is God's word. Her peace and reconciliation are not just the absence of war; they are guarantors of God's presence. God is the source of her peace, and its true abode is the hearts of men. True peace is fully realized only in God, and must be the object of man's permanent search. Peace cannot be found apart from God. In no sense is it the sole possession of those who are intelligent, rich, and powerful; they must attain it the same way as the foolish, the poor, the powerless. Peace is God's gift to all.

As long as there are the poor, the deprived, the imprisoned, and those discriminated against (through no fault of their own), the world cannot be at peace. Peace is available equally to all, to all nations and countries, without special favor. It belongs, properly, to the community of all mankind. It is not conditioned by one's strength or power, but only by God. Peace is an ultimate truth: it is justice for all.

Those who seek peace through social or political revolution will not find it, unless they have first found God's peace in their hearts. It cannot be captured at a conference table. In Međugorje it is said that a man stands tallest on his knees. In short, the search for peace is the search for God.

The most enthralling game the devil plays with man is war, which is his game: a time when decent, honest, and good people give themselves over to hate, destruction, and tragedy. This "game" does not begin in peace; neither does it end in peace. It begins and ends with the devil. Peace is established only by God.

The bishops of the United States, as well as our Holy Father, John Paul II, are engaged in a crusade for peace in our time, when speaking on abortion, social issues, issues of morality. They, and many others "on whom my favor rests," are today's prophets of our Lord Jesus Christ and his Mother, Mary. The words of peace spoken by God, by Mary, by the visionaries in Međugorje, and by people of good will throughout the world will be fulfilled by the power of God, when he conquers the world for Jesus Christ.

This peace is universal. It includes everybody and everything: the soul, the mind, the body, the spirit of each person, each family, of every race, color, religion, culture, country, and age.

Our Lady is bringing this peace to Christians, and Christians in turn are called to bring it to all the world. We believe that man will finally find peace when he surrenders to and reconciles himself with God.

Vjera (Faith)

In a seemingly endless search to understand himself, man reaches out in every direction, but his reach is too short, his grasp too weak, to seize full understanding of the meaning of his existence. However, God extended his hand to man through Jesus Christ, God's ever-present and extended hand to man, through the prophets and the fathers of the Church in the history of humanity. Faith, conversely, is man's extension of his hand to God.

"If anyone thirsts, let him come to me; let him drink who believes in me. Scripture has it: 'From within him rivers of living water shall flow'" (Jn 7:37-38). Jesus left his native village because he was "too much for them," and "he did not work many miracles there because of their lack of faith" (Mt 13:58). Our prayers, likewise, and requests for his help are inhibited by our lack of faith. Every time Our Lady is asked to help in healing a sick person, she asks for prayer, penance, and faith. Lack of faith is the root cause of man's self-destruction, and when a man chooses not to believe, it is a cause that God will not overwhelm.

Mirjana once said: "God cannot take it anymore!" This is very simple human talk, but it was said with transcendental, divine knowledge. It is Mirjana's expression of what she sees in the world, but it proceeds from God's experience with man as God revealed it to her (about you and me). Thus her words must be taken seriously. God is greatly displeased with our sinful behavior, and "without faith, it is impossible to please him" (Heb 11:6).

"This is the work of God: have faith in the One he sent" (Jn 6:29). Faith is a gift from God, but faith has vanished in many people. God holds no place in many hearts, and the results are inevitable. The soul and the spirit are impoverished, the mind is confused, meaning and goals are lost and confounded. The past is bloody and sad; the future is bleak. Our Lady, however, wants to bring us light and hope and comfort. Our Lady has come to waken our slumbering souls and spirits, to waken our faith in the One whom he sent.

The Word of God first came into our world in his creation of man "in his image" (Gen 1:27). In freedom, the first man decided to disobey God by eating fruit from the forbidden tree; thus he turned away from God. Later, the new Word of God was incarnated and came into the world in the person of Jesus Christ to restore peace – the initial unity and harmony between God and man – by being totally obedient to our Father. Now, in our time, Our Lady brings us the same Word of God, to be incarnated within us – to be as real in us as it is in her. Thus God celebrates eternal Christmas with man.

Mary has again brought the Word of God into the world so that man can say a momentous yes to the Word, as she did. Saying yes signifies personal surrender to God, in faith, for the Word of God is God himself. Somewhat as the Word, Jesus Christ, was born in Mary, it can be born in us. We thereby become a new creation, as the Creator means us to. The process is a real, personal liberation whereby man does not imprison himself in himself, but willingly reinstates God as the core or center.

(This is exemplified by the master of a merchant ship who came to Međugorje, after a 26-year lapse from the Church, to receive the sacrament of reconciliation. He explained it very simply: "I have seen all the world, and acquired wealth, but this has not satisfied me. I had to come here, and now I am happy!")

When man puts himself at the center of things, his power works against him and oppresses him. For him, "truth" becomes an attempt to justify his selfishness and his freedom to enslave himself, because he is unable to find the true way and the basic meaning of the world. Despite all revolutions, achievements and technical breakthroughs, and new knowledge in all fields, man is still forced to face the truth – the fact – of death. Thus life has become more tragic for him than ever before, because he has tried harder than ever before to dismiss – "account for" – the certainty of death.

The only alternative is faith in God and surrender to him (even though it is motivated by failure and desperation). God offers us his hand through Jesus and Our Lady, who brings her Son into the world again, making every new day a new Christmas, a new opportunity for conversion. God wills that every road in our lives lead to redemption, that every human effort meet the ultimate success, that every defeat and sacrifice contribute to final victory, that our death become new life.

History and experience show that, without God, freedom does not lead man to meaningful fulfillment of earthly and mundane ideals. Life without God instills no hope of surpassing human limitations. Those who are rich, or learned, or powerful – "successful" – are not content with their accomplishments, in fear they see their limitations. Consolation comes only through faith in God. Faith, moreover, does not deprive a person of dignity; it gives man purpose and hope both in living and dying.

The predicament of the modern world seems to indicate that man has gone as far as he can go on his own. As he wanders through the darkness of his world, he finds nothing that his mind can settle upon, except fear of self-destruction.

Our Lady of Međugorje seeks to bring us real faith, real meaning, and put us in touch with God and ourselves.

Molitva (Prayer)

"Our Lady prays." This seems to be the most appropriate statement about Our Lady whom the visionaries came to know in Međugorje. Christians have known Our Lady as God's mother and servant since the beginning in Nazareth. But the children and pilgrims of Međugorje emphasize "Our Lady who prays." Indeed, the very way of life in Međugorje calls for prayer. Everything that is said or done there can be described as a form of prayer, which Our Lady leads and urges everyone to follow. When Fr. Janko Bubalo asked Ivan Dragičević what he and Our Lady do during the visitations, he answered: "We pray together."

In early 1982 Our Lady was seen (by pilgrims and priests) in a posture of prayer before the cross on the hill of Križevac. When Fr. Vlašić asked the visionaries to ask Our Lady if it was she who was on the hill and if she was praying, Our Lady told the visionaries: "It is easily understandable that I should pray at the foot of the cross, which is the sign of salvation. My Son suffered on the cross, and redeemed the world on the cross. Salvation came from the cross."

In answer to a question from a priest about the necessity of forming a prayer group in his parish, she said: "There is need for a prayer group not only in his but in all parishes. Spiritual renewal is necessary for the entire Church."

In an interview with Vicka (March 15,1982), Fr. Tomislav asked her: "Do you experience Our Lady as one who gives graces or as one who prays to God?" Vicka answered promptly: "As one who prays to God."

In the same interview, Fr. Tomislav asked about the position of Our Lady's hands when she prayed, whether they are extended toward the visionaries and the crowds, or toward God. Vicka said that Our Lady's hands are extended up, toward God, and her palms are also turned up, toward God.

Many pilgrims to Međugorje have asked the children to ask Our Lady if prayer has the same efficacy, whether said in the church in Međugorje or in other churches, and the answer from Our Lady is that the efficacy varies, according to a person's fervor.

According to the children, Our Lady's response to all requests for healing can be summarized as: "I cannot heal you; only God can heal you. But pray to be healed and I will pray with you. Believe firmly, fast, and do penance, and I will intercede. God, of course, helps everybody; but I am not God."

Once, when Mirjana visited a sick man in a hospital, she asked if he wanted her to pray that he might be cured. Agitated, the man responded: "Are you crazy? I carry this cross for the salvation of the world. Please don't take it from me."

Not everyone who comes to Međugorje asks for physical healing, but everyone leaves Međugorje in an enhanced physical state, and certainly much happier, because their experience in Međugorje has caused them to grow in faith and prayer. More than physical cures, people search to heal their faith, their souls.

When a priest asked the visionaries to ask Mary whether we should pray to Jesus or to her, the response was: "Pray to Jesus. I am his Mother, and I intercede with him, but say all your prayers to Jesus. I will help you pray, but the strength of your prayers is more important."

Those who live in this world are not the only ones in need of prayer. When Our Lady showed the children Purgatory, she told them: "These people are anxious for your prayers and sacrifices."

Whenever Our Lady has been asked (through the children) to supply a special need, her answers have always been the same: There are no special prayers for special needs. Penance and prayer are the conditions for healing both the body and the soul. Nevertheless, people may mention a particular need or problem when they pray either for themselves or others. Every time we pray, Mary intercedes in our behalf.

Among some of the faithful there is the misunderstanding that Our Lady recommends praying only the seven Our Fathers, Hail Marys, Glorias, and the Credo. According to the visionaries, Our Lady recommends this form of prayer in addition to the prayers prescribed by the Church. Frequently, she recommends saying the rosary, and she emphasizes that every prayer is pleasing to God. She insists that the prayers she says with the children do not conflict with the time appointed for the Eucharistic celebration.

This, then, is Our Lady whom the six children came to know in Međugorje, Our Lady who prays with us and for us and who calls us to adopt the habit of daily prayer for all our intentions.

Prayer is the way we associate with her and communicate with God. For Christians, certainly, prayer is like being home. It is the most honorable, prestigious status a person can occupy. Prayer transports us to proximity with God himself, and Mary, and all God's saints – little short of where we've been destined to be.

When a human being does not pray, he relinquishes companionship with God – puts himself beyond God's reach. He enters a state of wandering, where even God consents to be powerless. Truly, such a person is lost in himself.

I was told the following by a man who had wandered far.

Every time I think about the days when I searched for happiness in bars, on the streets, in drugs, I feel sharp pain throughout my body. But the day I knelt in confession and prayed in the church at Međugorje is the happiest day in my life.

Now I am at peace. God and every human being have become my friends. Now the whole world is mine.

When Christians pray, they are home with God and Our Lady, wherever they may be. This is the way of life in Međugorje.

You, dear reader, must not think you are excluded from our prayer. You who have visited Međugorje are part of the spiritual River Jordan that flows past the Mother of God to nourish every parched corner of the world with "living water." In Međugorje, the priests, sisters, parishioners, and pilgrims pray for all who have come here. And those who have not been able to make this pilgrimage should know that all their sufferings and concerns are remembered in our prayers.

Even if you do not believe, if you do not have faith in God, the parish of Međugorje, together with the Mother of God, prays that God may speak to you.

The pastor, Fr. Tomislav, expresses the sentiment best: "Wherever you live, wherever you come from, we in Međugorje pray for you."

Post (Fasting)

Fasting – a strange-sounding word, a strange thing to do. It is foreign to our mentality, to the modern mind-set.

"Our supermarkets are filled to overflowing," we say, in effect, "and we have enough money to buy whatever they offer; so fasting is meaningless. Consuming means jobs for more people – prosperity. What's leftover, in food or money, could be given to the poor."

This line of thinking, besides being injurious to those who follow it, is as wrong as can be. Food is not the question. The poor are not the question. Money is not the question. You and I are the question.

Everything devolves upon the individual, his and her values and conception of reality, on you who are reading these lines and on me who is writing them. Look at it this way: we are running our race of life and God is watching our performance before he makes his awards. In running, we know, our feet leave the earth, for split seconds at a time but continuously. Unless a runner is thus detached from the earth, he cannot run very fast; so he has no business running a race. God – like a track coach – wants us to perfect our stride in this all-important race, to free ourselves from earthly, material goods (as much as we can), to develop spiritual fitness.

In itself, fasting has no value, no special meaning; but in the service of faith, it strengthens faith. When we fast, we control ourselves; and when we have control of ourselves, we can give ourselves to God, and to others as well.

Our Lady, unhappy that the practice of fasting has almost disappeared in the Church, wishes that it be revived: that every believer fast on Fridays, subsisting only on bread and water. This wish is corollary to her counsel of repentance and pertains to the necessity of reparation. Throughout the period of the visitations at Međugorje, prayer and fasting have constantly been emphasized as the most important preliminary to conversion and the surest way to obtain cures from illness. In effect, Our Lady prescribes faith, prayer, and fasting as the best "medicine" for every infirmity.

Those who are unable to fast because of their illness should substitute another form of penance, but those who are healthy cannot substitute: they must fast from food and drink.

ECUMENISM

The six visionaries all say Our Lady has told them that, in God, differences do not exist among his people; therefore diversity in religion need not separate people. Differences arise in the mundane world only because people isolate themselves. Every person, she says, must be respected, despite his or her particular profession of faith. No religious person should be held in contempt, if he or she is sincere in his or her profession.

God presides over all religions as a king controls his subjects, through his priests and ministers. Mary emphasized, however, that Jesus Christ is the only mediator of salvation.

Is there an essential difference among, say, Catholics and Protestants – in belonging to and praying in a particular church or community? The Virgin answered:

It is not equally efficacious to belong to or pray in any church or community, because the Holy Spirit grants his power differently among the churches and ministers. All believers do not pray the same way. It is intentional that all apparitions are under the auspices of the Catholic Church."

Again, Our Lady warned against condemning a person for sincerely holding a counter belief, and emphasized that such a person must be respected. Such disdain is especially prevalent in rural areas, and should not be countenanced. Once, while I was in the "vision room" in Međugorje, a young couple approached me and asked if they might speak to the children. Marija was standing next to me, and I said: "She is one of them." Joy immediately came over their faces – the joy of finding something precious at last. After they had conversed, Marija told me they were a Serbian Orthodox couple, originally from Belgrade, who lived and worked in Germany, and had come to Međugorje "to pray to Our Lady and to talk to us." Marija was almost ecstatic because their wish had been fulfilled.

In October of 1981, Fr. Ivica Vego, a priest from Mostar, asked Marija to put three questions to Our Lady, as follows:

1. What will happen in and to Poland? "There will soon be great conflicts there, but in the end, the righteous will triumph." Later that year, conflicts arose, but it is still too early to say that the righteous have prevailed.
2. Will the "case of Herzegovina" be resolved satisfactorily? "The problem will be resolved. There is a need for prayer and patience."
3. The third question pertained to the antagonism between the West and the East, and Our Lady said that the people of Russia will come to glorify the Lord. The West, she said, despite its technological prowess, behaves as if it has created everything that is worthwhile and thinks it has preempted God in the process.

Marija flushed when Fr. Ivica tried to learn more about the future of the West (this, apparently, impinged upon the "secrets"), and the subject was dropped.

PART 3
INTERVIEWS AND TESTIMONIES

Fr. Zrinko Čuvalo celebrating his First Mass
at Proboj on 11 August 1963

*This picture of Fr. Zrinko Čuvalo and these pages of
interview with him are in recognition of our deepest
respect and gratitude for the man that he was.*

XII

A FIRST ENCOUNTER
The Phenomenon of Apparitions

Franciscan Father Zrinko Čuvalo was born in Vitina, some 20 kilometers from Međugorje, in 1936. He was ordained to the priesthood in 1963 and as a dedicated pastoral worker, has served various parishes throughout the region of Herzegovina. Father Zrinko was present during the critical days of the beginning of the visions and was the first priest whom Marinko Ivanković told that something was happening to a group of children in Bijakovići (village at the base of the Hill of the Apparitions).

In addition, he was the first to actually talk to the children, which makes him a direct witness to all initial events as well as subsequent ones. Readers will find in his answers frank comments, a strong testimony of honesty and a living experience which affords a better insight into the development of events in Međugorje through the testimony of this priest.

Father Svetozar: Father, I would like for you to describe briefly – in your own way – the pattern of your belief from the moment when you first heard what Marinko told you to the moment when you actually began to strongly believe in the visions in Međugorje.

Father Zrinko: First, I am going to briefly explain my initial reaction. When I first heard about it from Marinko, I took no special stand toward it, but I simply took it as a news, the news which – if you like – never surprised me as much as it normally should. In fact, at that moment, I reacted pretty coolly, neither contemptuously, nor enthusiastically, but simply: "What can be – why should it not be."

That it can be, I have always believed, but for it to happen here, was something strange but not impossible. So, I simply acted accordingly. While Marinko was talking, I kept silent and at the conclusion made only this simple remark: "Thank God, go about your business, we shall see, we shall hear."

Then I went to bed. But during the night and the next day the news began to upset me. The next day I was not calm. I was worried. How could I have reacted to such news in such a way? How could I have so superficially passed over it? How could I have missed it?!

This can be better understood in the context of what Dragica Ivanković, Marinko's wife, told me two days later: "Where on earth are you?! Are you human? Are you a priest? Whatever are you? As if it didn't affect you at all?"

And it pinched me that night and the next day although I didn't know whether it was true or whether it was just a fraud or a common story of children's intrigues or morbid state. I thought of nothing else but that news and the way I took it, I mean so coolly. I did not come out against it – no, I didn't, nor did I accept it as something true.

You see, I could say the same even today as concerns those children. Not only today but all this time I have been fighting against myself and I cannot be in the clear about what is happening with me, why, up to this day, those children have never interested me at all although everything happens through them. They are a medium, a bridge, and there is no crossing from one riverbank to the other except by that bridge. But you see, that bridge does not interest me at all and that is what amazes, what puzzles me.

To make it clearer for you I am going to give you another example. There's talk about those signs. I couldn't see that sign on the sun because I was not there, and I did not see any special signs at all. All I saw was that strange whiteness round the Cross on the second day of Father Jozo's trial. That was in the early morning hours. I also saw the fire that many were talking about. When I came out of the office and saw what people were looking at and my first reaction was that it was an ordinary bonfire, as our people call it, which they make on the eve of a holy day.

That was my first reaction and I was angry with those who had done it and scolded them in my mind. Even later, I still placed no importance to it even when I heard that there was no sign of burning left and most said there was no burning at all. If it is so that it was a strange flame, which it was – then it is a sign of some type after all, a visible sign. It needn't be a miracle, but it is a sign after all.

Father Svetozar: You mean it is not essential.

Father Zrinko: Yes, it is not essential. It is of no importance. For me they are hardly of any value in relation to the events, to the happenings in Međugorje. You see, for instance, that fire or that whiteness never touched me in my faith during those two-and-a-half years. It is not a significant measure.

Here is what first touched me after that disappointment I had experienced to some extent on the Hill when I was for the first and only time present at the vision on Saturday, June 27.

Father Svetozar: Disappointment?

Father Zrinko: Yes. Disappointment in what I had expected to see and what I really saw during the vision. I didn't experience anything divine or supernatural and that's why I was disappointed. I gave to Fr. Jozo the recorded conversation I had with the children immediately after the vision. Then I gave each child a short question and after we had heard it together and when I told him my impressions, we both regretted, our not having gone there and telling the people: "Stop going to the hill!" Simply, forbidden it to all and dispersed the crowd.

Also, the disappointment resulted from what we had seen on the faces of those people who had been coming. For example, when I was going up the hill I heard one blaspheme God and Our Lady because he couldn't catch up with the children. Another abused God and Our Lady for not having appeared to him and I said to him: "I wouldn't appear to you myself, let alone Our Lady!"

That attitude of the people was repulsive. They pass by the church in a hurry. We stand in front of the church, nobody says to us: "Praised be Jesus and Mary! Father, how are you?" or "Is the church open?" Nothing doing! Instead, they came back with their cameras and seemed void of any spiritual experience.

Genuine Signs of God's Presence

Father Svetozar: What happened next.

Father Zrinko: Look now! What woke me for the first time from that darkness which ensued, which was taking more and more possession of us – both Fr. Jozo and me? What was the first light that flashed up in that darkness? For me, it was not the events there on the Hill, nor was it that whiteness round the Cross, but a meeting with a woman. One morning when I came to the church for the morning prayer and the Mass, a woman was waiting at the gate. She took me presently by the hand and said: "I'd like to confess." I replied: "Wait a minute." I went to open the church, but she came after me and said: "I'd like to confess." I answered: "But for God's sake, woman, don't you see, I'm going to open the church, can't you wait until after the morning prayer."

Namely, we used to say the morning prayer first and then to come out ten minutes or so before the Mass to hear confessions if there were any. She said again: "I'd like to have it done right away. I'm in distress." More kindly I answered: "All right if you insist." She came down on her knees, trembling and shaking all over. Whatever is the matter? What is the big trouble? And then I heard her confession. Afterwards I called her to the office, we had a talk and she gave a written statement to the office. Therefore, I am allowed to talk about it now.

It was about this: The woman was barren. She did everything to have a child. She made different promises to God, she fasted, she went on pilgrimages but remained childless after all, although she was still relatively young; she had been married for about fifteen years. And when she heard of the visions, she abused Our Lady: "Our Lady! Nonsense! If she existed at all, she should hear me. How many shrines have I visited barefooted, how much have I fasted" But the next Sunday she went to Mass and when she came to the church she hardly found courage to go in as if something had petrified her. Once in the church she was seized by anguish so that the other women had to lead her out of the church. Her husband took her home. Namely, when she saw Our Lady's statue in the church she was simply blocked. When she came home she asked in the middle of the night to go and confess. The husband did not let her go: "How could you go at this time of the night and bother the friars!"

And it was this woman's breakdown that enlightened me in my darkness that God must have a hand in this regardless of those doubts of ours and of what we were saying, for this was a sign enough for itself, a moral sign which was much clearer to me than the fire. You see, this one, we would say, seemingly common trifle, enlightened me more and kept shining to me more than the Hill, more than the fire on Crnica or that whiteness of the Cross.

Father Svetozar: Is there perhaps some other detail or a sign that later tended to lead you into a deeper understanding of those events?

Father Zrinko: For me the only genuine sign was when people adopted a spirit of penance, a spirit of conversion. A certain attitude and atmosphere of faith prevailed in this particular place and for me that was a sign.

Well, one can do penance and become a convert in other places as well; just the thing the government officials kept telling us at the meetings. They used to say: "Everybody has a church, priest, sacraments, Mass, Rosary, Fridays; let them go to their churches." This was what we, too, if you like, used to say, as well, at those times: "Go home and say your prayers, for your parish church stands empty and you come here beating the thorns about the hill."

Yet, after all we must admit that the Spirit came here and it was not forced. Well, it followed a priest's call, but we know that every priest calls to penance, to conversion almost every Sunday, but here the response was different.

The fact that here the people simply stuck to that Spirit was a sign for me, a sign that I couldn't fail to see. No more painful did I find those things I referred to earlier than the fact that people could not see these signs of conversion.

The Struggle of the First Days and the Search for the Truth

Father Svetozar: Fr. Zrinko, do you realize that at the beginning it was very difficult for some people to understand the skepticism of the priests?

Father Zrinko: I realize that it had to be difficult but we had to be that way. We had to be very critical indeed. We knew what the future had in store for us. When you hear the conversation I had with the children when I met them for the first time, you will see that I warned them to tell the truth. "One day shall we all together – including you my little boy – stand our trial," I said. "Now don't think that they are going to put you to prison now and try you; you shall appear before the church court. This is not a laughing matter." Now I am sorry that we do not have those tapes to hear them.

We were aware of our responsibilities from the very beginning. Regardless of whether it was truth or lie, it was bound to come on the carpet one day where we would be the most responsible. Therefore we behaved accordingly.

On the first Sunday when we addressed the congregation and every time when we spoke to the people we directed them toward the values of the Gospel and the Church. We discouraged them from aimless search for signs. At times perhaps we would say what we maybe didn't mean or want to.

We were all in fear. We had to be in fear just because of that future, of what was to come. No matter what it was, whether a plus, whether a minus, we were in fear. I think every man would find himself in fear, in anxiety at that moment.

Mind you, in this anxiety it pained us to see that people of our kind and rank, I mean clergy and sisters, were not truly with us. We wondered why they should run ahead of us. Sometimes I would even take my stand at the gate and entreat the visiting sisters to go to the convent and change to civilian dress. This is what I told our friars who walked up the Hill. This was not because of my disbelief but simply we were in fear that they would only too readily accuse a priest or sister, no matter whether you were for or against it.

Father Svetozar: But once you said that you had been open after all. What did you mean by that?

Father Zrinko: We were open to that happening, to that possibility and to what followed. We didn't know what it was but we kept the door open to let in whatever it was. We neither obstructed nor checked it, although Fr. Jozo had it on the tip of the tongue to say to everyone as he said to me once: "Go and disperse it!"

But we did not disperse the crowd, we didn't tell them not to go to the Hill but we grieved: Why go up there? Is there anywhere else but to go up there? But to tell you the truth, we were powerless and out of everything. The people did not pay any attention either to the church or to the priests. The children were not close to us. I remained the same. I am strict in my nature. I have always been that way.

We were very cautious, maybe too cautious, just out of fear, just out of the anxiety we found ourselves in. This is what I want to underline.

Yet, it is equally true that we were open maybe you don't see it because on the surface we were cautious, too cautious perhaps out of apprehension, out of the anxiety we were facing. That anxiety was not only because of the crowds, because of various questions, because of a time strait, but rather an anxiety within us. When you see something coming at you, you do not know what it is, how to take your stand, how to defend yourself, how to receive it, how to classify it. That I call anxiety: you see something coming, you don't know what it is and when it comes, you don't know whether it will crush you.

Father Svetozar: Fr. Zrinko, why did Doctor Vukšić, a very respected doctor from Ljubuški, a nearby town, come to Međugorje?

Father Zrinko: He came out of mere curiosity, for when these events became known everyone began coming: politicians, the police, priests, doctors – they all were coming and many, many other peoplé as well. Doctor Vukšić came, my brother Marijan who is also a doctor came, too. There were other doctors, as well.

Father Svetozar: Did Doctor Vukšić meet the children during those first days?

Father Zrinko: I do not know. I only recall that he told me something like this: I tell you it can't be from a drug. It was impossible for them to be drugged in such a short time, to such an extent, as to have hallucinations. You can easily tell those who are under the influence of a drug. I didn't discuss it with him any further. I knew his good reputation and that was enough for me.

Meeting with the State Authorities

Father Svetozar: Fr. Zrinko, what happened at the first meeting you and Father Jozo had in Čitluk with the representatives of the state authorities on the day when the children were at Cerno on June 30, 1981? I am interested in the elements of that meeting.

Father Zrinko: The officials from the government in Čitluk wanted to warn us that a lot of people were gathering up there on the Hill, that politically it was becoming very dangerous, that various elements were coming there, anything might happen, that it might bring harm to the region, the people and so it should be stopped as soon as possible. In short, it finished up with this cry of theirs: "Look, if they only wanted to keep within the church, if they were in the church, we wouldn't mind their never coming out of it."

Then we said that we priests had nothing against their being in the church, for if there is anything religious about it, it shall remain and end as such.

However, when the Mass was to be celebrated in the church, they came and asked for the Mass to be cancelled. The Mass seemed to have become even a bigger problem for them than the Hill itself. This might interest you. They wanted us to discontinue with the holy Mass. So they kept saying that there is nowhere a holy Mass celebrated in the evening. Mass is always celebrated in the morning. I said to them: In the Bible we have the Last Supper not the last breakfast.

Father Svetozar: As early as at that meeting both the medical examination and the health of the children were discussed as well. What was said about that?

Father Zrinko: We didn't bring the subject up at all but only set forth our difficulties and tried to assure them somehow that they had nothing to be afraid of since we bore the brunt rather than them. We tried to assure them that the matter was purely religious, one which might have bad effects only on the faith. I said plainly: "What negative could there be for you in all that? Should there be anything negative it will only befall us. It will sully the honor of the Church and the parish priest and not that of the sociopolitical organizations. Therefore, we are more upset and concerned about this matter than you are and therefore, we are going to inquire into this matter, for we do not know what it is about."

This was the difference between the authorities and us: they neither mentioned nor allowed for the possibility of revelation or supernatural intervention, but we did: the possibility exists. We refused bluntly their "Church teaching" of "No miracles after Jesus." We said that there had always been and would be miracles. "But," we said, "we do not know what this is. We shall see." We encouraged them: "We should open the eyes and see. We are going to investigate everything thoroughly. We do not know the children, we shall see what the children are like. We cannot judge everything. The experts will appraise what the children are like: whether they are hereditarily encumbered, whether they are sick, whether they are drugged – which is not excluded – whether they are being manipulated."

I also put in – I do not know whether directly or indirectly – this question: "Has the state security service any information or indication that it could be a manipulation from a third party?"

Father Svetozar: You asked for their help, then?

Father Zrinko: Yes! We were very cautious about the possibility of drugs and whether the children were perhaps being unknowingly manipulated.

That was what concerned Father Jozo even more than the drugs. As to drugs, Doctor Vukšić told me that it was out of the question. I concluded: If it is not drugs, then it must be something else. You know what I thought of: First, I thought that the enemies of the Faith had a hand in this pie, you see, that it might be an act of the militant atheism.

We were also saying at this point that the children should be examined in order to determine what they were really like. We were not qualified to pass opinion on the children and this was an important point: neither we, as priests, nor they, as politicians, could judge at that exact moment, whether the children were sane or not, whether they were drugged or not. In this respect, we were lay-men... both us and them.

Our approach was that first we must see what exactly it is that we are dealing with and then, only then, when we find it out, could we pass our opinion on the matter. Until then, we advised to leave the children in peace and proceed without tension and fuss. Our intention was to calm the situation.

Father Svetozar: For me, this meeting with the authorities is very interesting. It seems to me that it has given a direction to the further development of events in Međugorje...

Father Zrinko: You are correct. Not only that meeting but all the meetings which followed and all those events began to take strange turns which were always surprising to us. Actually, it seemed that we were all actors – the SUP (Secretariat for Internal Affairs), the Municipality, the sociopolitical organizations and those of us who were priests. It seemed that everything was acting somehow contrary to our plans, wishes and attitudes. Everything went differently and what is so interesting is that it tended to be so all of the time.

Actually, the authorities elected to take just what suited them. They never so much as thought that it might be a vision and that we might allow for it to be true. They adopted that curious standpoint, claiming it as a teaching, 'No miracles after Jesus'.

Father Jozo had been giving them a lesson in catechism on the matter for at least 45 minutes. Finally, one of the officials cut him short and replied with a blaspheme, adding sharply, "We have had enough of catechism. We haven't come here for you to give us a lesson in Church teaching. We have come here to reach an agreement with you."

Then I interposed: "What can we agree upon? We aren't gods to tell God what to do. If it is from God, neither you nor we – nobody – will be able to prevent what is happening. If it comes from the devil, it will only fall on our heads and then you will have nothing to be afraid of, for you can only cheer for joy over our dilemma." This was exactly what I told them.

After that, it began to seem that everything was going past us, all of us, independently, just going on its own way. We seemed to be only in service of all those happenings; it looked as though we were all being ferried and rowed across a river – all of us.

Looking back, perhaps it may seem strange that we, priests, should have taken such a resistant attitude: Father Jozo and myself. To everyone, we, the local priests of the parish, appeared to be absolutely against the visions and to even ignore the events as much as possible.

Actually, for the first few days, everybody seemed – in some way or another – to have accepted or at least allowed for the possibility except for us.

Dragica, Marinko's wife, finally came and fired away at me. She told me to my face and with much honesty that everybody was up there – from the police to the mayor, doctors, priests, friars, bishop's secretary and all sorts of people. She asked pointedly, "Only you are keeping back. You, who should be first. No sign of you. Shame on you! What are you here for anyway? You, unbelievers! You should be chased away!"

Father Svetozar: And what did you do?

Father Zrinko: I only tapped her on the shoulder and said: "Dragica, calm down, you will see one day and you will know, too, why we had to be the last."

Personal Attitude

Father Svetozar: And now I would like to ask you a ticklish question. I would like to know how you, in your personal life, experienced what was sought for in Međugorje, those messages, especially the messages of fasting, praying, penance and conversion?

Father Zrinko: The call to reconciliation, prayer, to penance, to conversion and fasting was a concrete call of the Blessed Virgin Mary which offered to the world something else, something more than the Hill, actually something in exchange for the Hill.

I believed from the very beginning, that if the Blessed Virgin Mary was appearing to the children, then she had a message, and the message cannot be anything else but the Gospel.

The Revelation is ended and the Revelation we have. Now we can only be warned of the failures in our attitude towards the Revelation and those who are opposed to it may come to believe in it. I understood the message in this context.

Nor is it important to me through whom that message is conveyed, whether through the children's mouth, or whether by people's plebiscite, spontaneously. That is not of decisive importance.

In fact, much of it has happened spontaneously. Seven Our Fathers is something that the children started of their own accord and which Mary blessed. And, now, how and why they started just this and not something else, I still believe that it may be said after all, that it is God's hand here and it comes from God.

For example, I remember Father Jozo calling the people at the first Mass to penance, to conversion, to prayer. It was at the beginning of the Mass, in the act of repentance. The idea was that whoever had opted for Christ would go to pray with him, go to fast, go with him into the desert, go fight the devil and conquer him.

So, right from the beginning, from the first day, one started with the values that had been guaranteed throughout Revelation, I took it, as I said, as a way I had known before.

The essential for me is this: Have these children ever had any experience, have they received anything from God, through Our Lady, in any way whatsoever? Has Our Lady intervened at all before those children, no matter how, be it only with one single sentence: "Go and tell those people down there to stop quarrelling, to make peace with each other and with God, because it is high time." That was enough for me.

Father Svetozar: Do you believe that Our Lady has intervened?

Father Zrinko: I am somehow inclined to believe it, not on the ground of the children's statements however, but on the ground of what followed, what was generated from those statements, from the children's story.

In my opinion, we should not rely too much on the children at every moment and in every detail. For example, I said to the Bishop and the others openly and aloud: "When the children say now this, now that, when they disagree, that does not astonish me. Bishop, if I were in their shoes, I would not always be clear! I would have to be vague sometimes! Why? How?"

Then I explained it to him. Supposing the children did receive something, then it is quite natural for them to think about it and interpret it in their own way, to clothe it in their own making, to convey some of their own thoughts as if these were Our Lady's. We shouldn't call it deception, for they are human after all.

That's what I suppose. How many people came asking for this, asking for that – well-intentioned and sometimes ill-intentioned! We humans remain humans. Children remain children. We can't expect them to become somebody else. They convey the message in the way they understand it so that sometimes, it's possible, when asked, to say what they think Our Lady might have said, reasoning simply: "I'm going to say what She might say about it" or "I suppose it was like that," or "As far as I remember She said it this way." In other words each of them gives these events some stamp of their own. But, there is no intent to deceive or mislead. Something similar could be said about the priests.

Fr. Jozo called to fasting and took Friday as a special day for doing penance. Fr. Tomislav began on his arrival to insist on a deeper and longer prayer, especially calling to strict fasting.

Father Svetozar: It is interesting that I myself have come to what you said now, that the role of the priests who were working in the parish, together with the whole Christian community, which was open to the Holy Spirit, was immense. You, the priests, gave to everything a right pastoral and spiritual direction.

Father Zrinko: As I said, we remained open, we were in suspense. What was to be expected? If it is really God's messenger who is coming, then he can't be bringing anything else but what God has already given, offered to the man. It can be nothing else but a warning, a rebuke, or an advice. What could we do then?

We saw what it was. We knew what the situation in the parish, in the world, in man in general was like. We saw what was missing and what had disappeared in the Christian world.

Prayer had disappeared, fasting had disappeared practically in the whole Church. The world understood the Church Reform to be a fast repeal. I often had a chance to hear at Confession: "What, hasn't fast been repealed?!"

Such a mentality was gaining ground. Prayer disappeared, it was banished by radio and television. Even the Mass was observed more as a custom. Young people already had their different interests and preoccupations. Quite often only religious customs were observed, the Mass and the like, while in other surroundings even the custom disappeared.

About the Pilgrims

Father Svetozar: Fr. Zrinko, you talked about your own experiences and feelings and now I would like you to tell me something about the people who came. How did they experience all those events and Our Lady's message and the message they found in Meðugorje?

Father Zrinko: It seems to me that after the first two or three months the people here experienced the same as I did. That is, we looked toward the Hill less and less. It is interesting to note that from September forward, hardly anyone, even of those who came from other parts, tried to go to the Hill or look there during the apparition.

Naturally, there always were the curious ones who had come for the first time and heard about the spinning cross and so they would keep staring there in the hope to see the cross spin around. However, most people simply sought God and experienced the presence of Our Lady in the church, in the sacraments. Indeed, most of those people came for a meeting with God, for a meeting with Our Lady, for evening service. It was not only the Mass, but also what preceded it. People came for the Rosary so readily and stayed for the Prayer for the Sick that followed, even those who were not ill and who did not need it. They simply stayed behind, they wanted to be together with Our Lady there. I got the impression that the people had formed an attitude similar to mine and that God was at work here. And in this process it became clear to me that the children were involved as instruments through which God was working.

Father Svetozar: I believe He works both through them and through the others.

Father Zrinko: Yes, He worked through everybody. After all it is God's business, how is not relevant to me at all, I mean through whom God works. What matters is that He does work!

I would like to illustrate this view of mine with an example which Father Zoran told me. When one of his pa-

rishioners came back to Chicago from Međugorje he told
Father Zoran about meeting a colleague of his who asked
him: "Where have you been?"

"In Međugorje."

"Well, what did you see there, did you see Our Lady?"
the colleague asked mockingly.

"Yes, I did, both God and Our Lady," replied the former.

What he meant was that he had experienced God here
and that he had not been deceived.

And this is exactly what people experience and what
gathers and keeps them together, and that is what brings
them here again and again. We say: "God is everywhere."
Yes, God is everywhere, but He is at work here in a special way.

Father Svetozar: Please continue.

Father Zrinko: When I started to analyze certain acts of
all possible authorities, starting from the communal authorities up to the federal ones in Belgrade, and from the
ones in Rome up to our local church authorities... I mean
all authorities who had any influence and importance
whatsoever, I realized that they all had acted in some
other direction and everybody tried – in their own way –
to turn the events into a track of their own liking.

How interesting! No matter what move they made, and
those moves were different, coming from different sides,
at different times, of different intensity – never did the
thing move the way it was tugged, but always in another,
unforeseen direction.

Yet, when you take it all together, you see it was
heading in one single direction that had been marked from
the beginning. No matter where you tugged, it always
went in it's own direction. For example, how much I re-

sented that guard, the rude acts barring the access to people, to cars, etc.! Later I said, once before some officials – that I should invite all the militia and the whole SUP of Čitluk to a barbecue, because what a mess it would have been, if it hadn't been for them!

You can imagine what a jam it would have been, if cars had been admitted. Or what might have happened, what it might have turned into, if they had not forbidden going to the Hill. Later I thought: "Well, folks, how shallow we are when we ask who organized all this." Once I intimated this to the Bishop when he came to Meðugorje: "If somebody had tried to arrange this, he would have never come upon the idea." We were all angry at what the adversaries were undertaking, and now I say, if it hadn't been for that, it seems to me that it couldn't have come to all this. What we have today, wouldn't be if it hadn't been for this. Now I come to the conclusion that God engaged them all – those in the SUP the municipal officials, the Bishop, the provincial, and those clergymen and friars who were always with us and those who even didn't let their parishioners come here – to make this possible.

Or for example, for the first Christmas, huge crowds of people were about to come. We were in big trouble how to accommodate so many people for that night, anything could happen. It was easy to suppose a thief, a robber, a provoking agent and all. We were panic-stricken. But God solved the whole problem by a heavy rain. Those who did come had to wade through knee-deep water on the asphalt road. Those who couldn't have a place in the church went back home and everything was solved.

At many a moment we were greatly worried over how everything was going to turn out and there were reasons for such worries every day. But when you sum up everything, it seems as if a director had taken his stand behind the stage, kept watching how everything was and then arranging everything.

You might fret as much as you liked, everything went its own course. For me that was a sign of God's hand, God's presence; that God managed it all, because man is not that clever. I was especially fascinated by the way God thwarted man's plans, his wits and power. Then you can't but see God's hand here. Here I felt God and the Blessed Virgin at work. Here God's hand was somehow visible to me. No matter how hard they tried, the enemies did not succeed in leaving the church without Mass for a single day.

Humanly viewed, Mass seemed impossible to celebrate. Father Jozo had been imprisoned. We had been put in quarantine and were not allowed to leave the house. Barricades had been erected and watched by guards. Nobody was allowed to approach the church. All the other priests had left. Yet, the Mass did start – with ten minutes delay – and not more!

Then the police let everybody go to the church and the Mass began. It was celebrated by a priest who I didn't know at all, Father Stanko Dodig, a Capuchin, a man from the village, guardian of a monastery in Rijeka. He had been called to preach in Sarajevo, and on his return he dropped in to see his mother. So the Mass was celebrated after all!

Everything that was undertaken, turned out well. Even now, all the difficulties and sufferings are words powerfully spoken and a calling to penance for all those who come here. It is a message which says: Either keep out or do penance. The whole environment of Međugorje directs to penance. The whole environment.

Departure of Father Jozo

Father Svetozar: How did you feel about Father Jozo's imprisonment.

Father Zrinko: How did I feel about it? I told the people when he was taken. It was difficult indeed. I could best illustrate this difficulty by saying that I was really sorry for having stayed behind, for not having gone myself. Later, I regretted it also several times that I was not in his place, simply because it was such a maltreatment.

Those days a few other people went to prison: Fr. Ferdo Vlašić (5,5 years), Fr. Jozo Križić (2,7 years), Mr. Ivan Ivanković (2 months), Mr. Gojko Ostojić (2 months), Mr. Pero Pehar (2 months) and Fr. Jozo Zovko (1,5 years).

I immediately sent a report to the Provincial and the Bishop about what had happened in which I said that it was absolutely out of the question, my being pastor in Father Jozo's (the real pastor) forced absence. In addition, I asked not to be made acting pastor either. This was adopted and so, before the Feast of the Nativity, Father Tomislav Vlašić got a decree to the effect of being appointed pastor.

Life went by. Many people did not know who the acting pastor actually was. We both knew what each of us had to do and it didn't matter who the pastor was.

Each time when somebody came asking for the pastor we would say: "He is in prison."

The adversaries were for me to be the pastor. First, because I never led the evening service. Second, I did not talk to the children, I did not come out on their behalf, did not represent them. I sought to be objective. Third, since the day when Mrs. Draga Ivanković came to me, I was regarded as being against the apparitions.

And, I guess the children did find me very stern, rude, not so meek as Father Jozo. Such a reputation of mine took air. Sometimes, it created difficulty for me. Finally, in January 1982, the Church authorities decided to appoint me acting pastor instead of Father Tomislav. I held this office until the end of August 1982.

A Look at the Međugorje Days

Father Svetozar: Is there anything special you would like to say about that time when you were acting pastor in Međugorje? Did any special things happen at that time which you stamped your personal hallmark on? I particularly refer to the development of events about the apparitions in Međugorje and about the coming of pilgrims.

Father Zrinko: There is no special hallmark to it. The only thing that I went by was not to ever try to put obstacles to God's action or to be such an obstacle myself. I let the things go their way taking care only lest something should creep in that wouldn't be in conformity to the discipline of the Church and to God's Revelation. That was the only thing I was sensitive about and watched vigilantly, the rest I left over to time and situation.

Father Svetozar: Your attitude to the people you were meeting was, something special, something that everybody noticed and that was conspicuous to everybody. Will you say something about that?

Father Zrinko: My attitude – harshness, impudence, inconsiderateness – struck everybody. I was aware of it. I was also aware of another fact: without it one could not make order and keep the matter serious. I simply could not allow people to do as they pleased. I wanted everything to remain on a decent level. That's why I used force, if it was necessary – and often it was – in terms of hard words and sharp behavior. I was fully aware that it did not befit a man, let alone a priest, but at that time I served Međugorje the way I felt I should serve it. Looking into the future I was deeply convinced that Međugorje would remain a spiritual oasis no matter how the visions were going to end, what attitude many people would assume. Međugorje would remain.

Father Svetozar: What are your memories of that time?

Father Zrinko: I say, it is hard to speak about personal dispositions and feelings. We shall leave it for some other time. I only know, and that was clear to everybody, that it was very hard for me, that I had to fight on four fronts: with the state authorities, Church authorities, with the parish and with the pilgrims.

Father Svetozar: I feel by your smile, though, that this time has remained as God's gift, in a pleasant memory, as a time which gives you peace.

Father Zrinko: Look here, when I was leaving Međugorje, those who witnessed it could see that I was indisposed, that something happened that had never happened before on similar occasions when I was leaving a parish: my eyes were full of tears. It was only then that they realized the depth of my feeling for them and for the place.

Father Svetozar: Fr. Zrinko, it is a general conviction that you, among others, were God's gift to Međugorje at that time with all your strong qualities and abilities and that you are a part of all that was happening there.

Father Zrinko: Once at a meeting the officials said and admitted this: "We all thought Zrinko was like this, Zrinko was like that, but Zrinko does not give way an inch from the line." They had expected me to give in and to break the whole thing up. Maybe I sometimes did look frivolous. Mistaking superficiality and lack of interest on my part, they thought (the people from the government): "Well, Zrinko is going to end all that." That's why they used to forgive me many things. I would have been locked up for what I said, if I had been somebody else.

Father Svetozar: Fr. Zrinko, these were the questions that I had wanted to ask you and that I had at heart. I know there are many of them which have remained unasked and therefore unanswered. Still I believe that we have touched upon the most important ones and that the readers will find in your answers a strong testimony and a living experience and will get a better insight into the development of events in Međugorje as I have got by listening to you.

I cannot help saying how much I was surprised by your readiness to say what you have at heart. In your face and in your words I am reading a strong belief in God, love for Our Lady and a desire to convey to others, not only by words but also by transfusion of your spirit, what you feel, believe and experience. Thank you!

Father Zrinko: Thank God!

Father Zrinko Čuvalo died of cancer June 1, 1991 and was buried at Humac, near Ljubuški.

Summer evening Mass at Međugorje, 2005.

St. James, Patron of the Međugorje parish

The Hill of Apparitions

| Pomegranate | Heather |
| (Punica granatum) | (Saturea montana) |

Two common plants growing on the hills around Međugorje

The Holy Mass on Križevac, 2005

Mother with children in prayer to the Mother in the parish church at Međugorje

St. Anthony

St. Leopold Bogdan Mandić, the Confessor

**Vicka, Jakov, Mirjana, Ivanka, Marija and Ivan during the
vision on the first anniversary of the Apparitions (1982)**

Ivan and Marija during an apparition

Vicka and Jakov during an apparition

Ivanka

Mirjana

†Fr. Slavko Barbarić

a painting by Aleksandr Zvjagin at Mother's Village

†Fr. Bono Krndelj

†Fr. Ivan Bradvica

Fr. Ivan Bradvica and Fr. Bono Krndelj lived in Konjic in the years after the war. They both died late in 2000 just a few weeks before Fr. Slavko.

**Bishop of Mostar, Msgr. Ratko Perić,
Sacrament of Confirmation in Međugorje, 2005.**

**Fr. Svetozar, Fr. Ivan, Fr. Viktor, Fr. Branimir, Fr. Kvirin, Fr.
Ivan, Fr. Petar, Fr. Slavko, Fr. Stanko**

Fr. Jozo Zovko

Fr. Tomislav Vlašić

Fr. Tomislav Pervan

†Fr. Leonard Oreč

Fr. Ivan Landeka

Fr. Branko Radoš

Fr. Ivan Sesar

†Fr. Ljudevit Rupčić

Fr. Stanko Vasilj

H. Do - šli smo Ti, Maj - ko dra - ga
E. We come to you, dear - est Moth - er

Fr Viktor Kosir

Sister Slavica

Sister Stojka

Sister Marina

Sister Auksilija

Sister Janja

Sister Ruža

Merciful Father's Community at Mother's Village

**Father Caroll Aiden and Mrs Kay Barry,
pilgrims and friends from Ireland**

The teaching of Archbishop of Split, Frane Franić, helped the
pilgrims to understand the words of Our Lady to the visionaries.

Archbishop emeritus of New Orleans, Philip Hannan, a friend
and one of the pioneer pilgrims from the US.

Jim Caviezel on pilgrimage to Međugorje

**Cardinal Bernardino Echeverria Ruiz giving
an interview to Fr. Slavko, June 1999.**

We will hear his will in the sacraments

Pray, pray, pray!

**Fr. Jozé Rodríguez Carballo, OFM, General Minister
of the Franciscan Order climbing Podbrdo**

Vicka speaking at the Youth Festival 2005

XIII

PRIESTS' TESTIMONIES

The Phenomenon of Međugorje
As Seen by Fr. Viktor Kosir
and Fr. Tomislav Vlašić

Frs. Zrinko Čuvalo and Viktor Kosir were the first priests to go to the site of the visions. Fr. Vlašić – on January 26, 1982 – interviewed Fr. Victor and queried him about his experiences during those first days. Later in the interview, Fr. Vlašić tells something about his own experiences in this connection.

After a congress of Franciscan friars at Široki Brijeg on June 26, 1981 Fr. Viktor invited Fr. Zrinko to visit Posušje, and he observed that "Fr. Zrinko was noticeably different – that is, unusually quiet or withdrawn – but he did not indicate what was on his mind." Soon after Fr. Zrinko's departure, Fr. Jozo came to Posušje on his way back from Zagreb, where he had been on a retreat, and on the morning of June 27 he went to Mostar, where his mother had been hospitalized, to visit her; and Fr. Viktor accompanied him. In front of the hospital they met Dragica Ivanković, who had gone from Međugorje to the hospital in Mostar to be treated for injuries she had sustained at work.

When Fr. Jozo approached Dragica to ask her about her injuries, she almost shouted at him: "Where have you been? You should go to Međugorje! Fr. Zrinko is all alone there – and Our Lady has appeared there!"

145

Neither priest knew what to make of her outbreak; nevertheless, they went to Međugorje, and the first words they heard were the housekeeper's: "Where have you been? Our Lady has appeared!" Fr. Zrinko then came and said: "I have something here for you," wherewith he gave them tapes of the conversation he had conducted with the children who said they had had the vision.

Unable to reach any conclusions after they had listened to the tapes, they summoned the children to the rectory to talk to them. While they waited for the children, Fr. Viktor asked Fr. Jozo if he knew them or anything about them; but neither priest knew anything about the children. In his conversation with the children, Fr. Viktor said, he looked for signs of mental illness or unbalance, external influence, deceitfulness, or the influence of drugs. "They seemed absolutely honest," Fr. Viktor said, "and I found no trace of religious imbalance. They seemed to be perfectly normal children. I discovered nothing that I could pinpoint as a lie, mental disturbance, or undue persuasion. However, I was still unable to make any kind of judgment."

The next day, June 28 (a Sunday), Fr. Viktor returned and, with Fr. Zrinko, Marija, and Jakov, went to the site of the alleged vision. "On my way to the hill," Fr. Viktor said,

> Marija and Jakov were walking with me when, suddenly, Marija's face turned bright red. "Look! Look! Look!" she said. Jakov did not say anything, but together they ran ahead at what seemed incredible speed. Marija wore a white blouse and a red skirt, so I could see her distinctly as she ran far ahead of me, almost seeming to fly. It was impossible for me to keep up with her.

The next day was the Feast of St. Peter, and Fr. Viktor returned to Međugorje "to be of some help." Fr. Jozo was not home that day. It was later learned that he had simply absented himself because he thought it would be better if he were not present.

When he reached the spot where the vision had appeared, and "when the time came," Fr. Viktor says,

they were praying Our Father, the Hail Mary, and the Gloria; and many people were standing near them. I was about ten feet away, and somewhat agitated. As I looked at their faces, I felt that the apparition – as they called it – had begun. I watched Jakov very carefully; he was looking downward and in front of him. After their "conversation" with Our Lady had ended, I approached Jakov and asked him where Our Lady had come from: from above, or the left or right? "I saw her right in front of me," he said. If he said he had seen her elsewhere, he would have had to move his head and I would know he was lying; but he did not, and so I concluded that he was not lying.

Then Marinko came to us, carrying a stone with a cross painted on it, and he asked: "Children, where did Our Lady appear?" and they all indicated the same spot and said: "There!"

We returned to the rectory to talk with the children, and I asked the children, individually: "How old did Our Lady seem to be?" and all the answers were "around 19 or 20." Jakov was the last one I asked. I brought him in front of the others and asked: "Jakov, how old would you say she is?" and he told me: "Around 20 years old." "You see," the others exclaimed, "we told you!"

Reflecting on this incident, Fr. Viktor says:

Their identical answers, when I questioned them separately, and their answer to Marinko's question about the exact position of the vision, convinced me that they were telling the truth. My intention had been to demonstrate that their versions contradicted each other and thereby discredit their allegations and preserve the parish from credulity and becoming a public laughingstock – Fr. Jozo, the children themselves, but primarily the Catholic faith. But they passed every test and removed every doubt. My stern inquiry was calculated to bring out the truth.

Fr. Viktor concludes:

My most significant experiences pertaining to the phenomena at Međugorje are Church-related, in administering the sacrament of reconciliation to pilgrims to Međugorje, then seeing their joy and enthusiasm. Of course, the changes in my parish are also significant. The parishioners are diligent in praying the seven Our Fathers, Hail Marys, Glorias, and the Angelus. I have been deeply moved by all this, and so has everyone else. For example, there is no one in Posušje who has gone to Međugorje once, because of the visions, but has not gone there again. Once, seventy-five young people from Posušje hiked the full seventy kilometers to Međugorje. And speaking of Fr. Jozo's homilies, they said, though they had known him well: "Rather than Fr. Jozo speaking, it was as if Jesus were speaking through him." Especially on Friday, the people hereabout observe the strictest form of fasting. The transformation has been wonderful; moreover, the people are aware of the profound change and their need to change. All this, of course, has been helped by what is heard from and about Međugorje, but the change is very real.

Fr. Tomislav Vlašić is, so to speak, the spokesman in Međugorje of Our Lady and the children; he is also the region's foremost liturgist. He came to Međugorje for the first time on St. Peter's Day (June 29), and Jakov was the first of the visionaries he spoke to. "He spoke to me very simply and openly", Fr. Vlašić says of his talk with Jakov,

> and was not devious in any way. I was soon convinced that he was undergoing some unusual experience, but I had no idea what it was. Next I spoke to Mirjana and asked her a few questions, but she was somewhat uneasy because they had just been interrogated by the police. She said that it had been like being in prison or with lunatics. When I asked her if she would return to the hill, she said she doubted it. "Probably I will not, because if they take me back to question me, I'll have a nervous breakdown." I mention this because, just a short time later, I saw her on the hillside, and when I asked her why she had changed her mind, she said: "When the time came to go there (to the hill), no one could have stopped me. There was no longer any question of going or not going."

Talking about the gathering of people on the hillside at the time of the vision, Fr. Tomislav said the people were praying, but the praying was unorganized. He therefore felt a need to bring the people to the church, to pray in the church, and to try to help them understand what had happened. After that I went to the house of Marinko Ivanković, and there I met five of the children. I spoke to them and received the firm impression that the children were healthy in every way. I noticed that they did not seem to be burdened or afflicted by any disorder, and they were not under the influence of drugs. All their reactions were normal.

Our Lady's Messages
Written Testimony by Fr. Tomislav
Given to Me in Međugorje
on April 22, 1983

I have been asked to say a few words about the messages of Our Lady at Međugorje, and though it is very, very difficult to relate all the circumstances, it is easy to state the messages. To relate them in full, I would have to have the soul of Mary, and her mentality. However, I will share with you what I have seen and what I have experienced in my soul, and I pray that all who read this will receive it as if it came from Mary herself.

To me, the greatest message of Mary at Međugorje is her very appearance. To the visionaries, she became visible and touchable. They listen to her, speak to her, sing and pray with her; and she enabled all of them to see Heaven, Hell, and Purgatory. Thus Heaven has been opened to us through Mary – everything that Jesus speaks of is brought before our eyes. In a person who receives this revelation in faith, everything is seen in a new and different light, and he becomes born again. In a sense, then, Mary's apparition gives the Church new birth.

Immediately after the apparition is the invitation to faith. After the apparition, the believer is invited to approach Jesus Christ and to conform his life to that of Jesus. Besides, Our Lady has expressly invited the world, through the visionaries, to renew its faith. She said to the visionaries: "The best prayer is the Creed." Again, when the sick, through the visionaries, asked Our Lady to help, she called upon them to fast and pray, and she emphasized: "It is most important that you believe!"

Mary does not appear in these apparitions as a "still" photograph or a moving-picture image. She appears as a loving Mother who, with trembling heart, calls to her children to travel the road to salvation. She repeatedly speaks to the children about the great tensions in the world and how close to catastrophe the world hovers. Nevertheless, she invites the world to peace and reconciliation. Indeed, on the third day – June 26, 1981 – she invited the world to find peace, but on the fourth day, Marija Pavlović saw a frightful black cross and Our Lady standing in front of it, with large tears coursing down her face. "Peace, peace, peace," she repeated, "reconcile yourselves!"

On one of the first days (the exact date is not known, because Fr. Jozo's notes mysteriously disappeared from his room), a group of pilgrims, together with the pastor, saw the word peace in the sky, written in bright letters. When the children asked her if she would be known by various names, she introduced herself as "Queen of Peace."

We know, at any rate, that peace in the world is possible only through God, and will be realized only if we conduct our relationships with our fellow men as the universal Mother does. She bears life, watches over it, and lives for it. She does not seek her happiness in others' pain.

Peace, therefore, cannot be attained without thorough-going conversion to the teaching of Jesus Christ: "You shall love the Lord your God with your whole heart, with your whole soul, and with all your mind... You shall love your neighbor as yourself." (Mt 22:37, 39) Such love, Our Lady tells us, is attained through prayer and penance.

She told the children to tell the people to pray, every day, seven Our Fathers, seven Hail Marys, seven Glorias, and the Creed (once). This is the minimum, together with the other Christian duties. "Some Christians," she observed, "are no longer believers because they do not pray."

On July 21, 1982 Our Lady told the children: "The world has forgotten the value of fasting and prayer. With fasting and prayer, wars could be stopped and natural laws suspended... Only the seriously ill are free from fasting, but fasting cannot be replaced by prayer and almsgiving, except by those who are ill." She also said: "You should pray and fast on behalf of the sick. It is easy for God to heal them, but it is not easy for man..."

In the spring of 1983, all the children seemed to concentrate on the work of conversion, and one of them stated the message of Our Lady in these words: "Hasten your conversion! Do not wait for the sign. It will be too late for nonbelievers to convert. For those who believe, this is the time to convert and deepen their faith."

Then, on April 20, 1983, the children saw Our Lady in tears, distraught by the plight of grievous sinners. She had tried her utmost, she said, but they would not convert.

Pray for them – pray everyday for them and do not wait. I need your prayers and penance."

Our Lady has not spoken at length about particular devotions. She has noted, however, that "all prayer is good if one prays with faith." Nor has she spoken about the sacraments generally, except to urge Christians to revive the habit of monthly confession: "Monthly confession would be healing medicine for the Church of the West. Whole provinces of the Church would be healed if believers would confess their sins once a month." Otherwise, she spoke of the sacraments as the "regular practice of the Church" and implied that she had called for them sufficiently "in my other apparitions."

Now, dear friend and reader, you have heard the simple, straightforward words of Our Lady – simple words essential for salvation. My wish is that readers do not accept them as mere information but, instead, "internalize" them, incarnate them, as Mary did when the angel appeared to her. Let these messages become essential parts of your life, and convey them to others as Mary hastened to tell Elizabeth the "good news." The world, we pray, will at last be cleansed from sin and, embraced by its Creator, will turn its face toward true happiness.

(signed) Fra Tomislav Vlašić O.F.M.

XIV

INTERVIEW WITH MIRJANA DRAGIČEVIĆ

By Fr. Tomislav Vlašić
Međugorje, January 10, 1983

Fr. T: Mirjana, we have not seen each other for some time, and I would like you to tell me about the apparitions of the Blessed Virgin Mary, and especially the events that are connected with you.

M: I have seen the Blessed Virgin Mary for eighteen months now, and feel I know her very well. I feel she loves me with her motherly love, and so I have been able to ask her about anything I would like to know. I've asked her to explain some things about Heaven, Purgatory, and Hell that were not clear to me. For example, I asked her how God can be so unmerciful as to throw people into Hell, to suffer forever. I thought: If a person commits a crime and goes to jail, he stays there for a while and then is forgiven – but to Hell, forever? She told me that souls who go to Hell have ceased thinking favorably of God – have cursed him, more and more. So they've already become a part of Hell, and choose not to be delivered from it.

Then she told me that there are levels in Purgatory: levels close to Hell and higher and higher toward Heaven. Most people, she said, think many souls are released from Purgatory into Heaven on All Saints' Day, but most souls are taken into Heaven on Christmas Day.

T: Did you ask why God allows Hell?

M: No, I did not. But afterward I had a discussion with my aunt, who told me how merciful God is. So I said I would ask Our Lady how God could...

T: According to what you've said, then, it's as simple as this: people who oppose God on earth just continue their existence after death, and oppose God in Hell?

M: Really, I thought if a person goes to Hell... Don't people pray for their salvation? Could God be so unmerciful as not to hear their prayers? Then Our Lady explained it to me. People in hell do not pray at all; instead, they blame God for everything. In effect, they become one with that Hell and they get used to it. They rage against God, and they suffer, but they always refuse to pray to God.

T: To ask him for salvation?

M: In Hell, they hate him even more.

T: As for Purgatory, you say that souls who pray frequently are sometimes allowed to communicate, at least by messages, with people on earth, and that they receive the benefits of prayers said on earth?

M: Yes. Prayers that are said on earth for souls who have not prayed for their salvation are applied to souls in Purgatory who pray for their salvation.

T: Did Our Lady tell you whether many people go to Hell today?

M: I asked her about that recently, and she said that, today, most people go to Purgatory, the next greatest number go to Hell, and only a few go directly to Heaven.

T: Only a few go to Heaven?

M: Yes. Only a few – the least number – go to Heaven.

T: Did you ask about the conditions for a person to enter Heaven?

M: No, I didn't; but we can probably say what they are. God is not looking for great believers but simply for those who respect their faith and live peacefully, without malice, meanness, falsehood.

T: This is your interpretation, your understanding?

M: Yes. After I talked to Our Lady, I came to that conclusion. No one has to perform miracles or do great penance; merely live a simple, peaceful life.

T: Did you see Hell?

M: No, I did not. I did not want to.

T: You did not want to see it?

M: I did not.

T: Purgatory?

M: I didn't see Purgatory either. Just Heaven. But Our Lady described Purgatory as I told you – with levels.

T: Well, besides Heaven, Hell, and Purgatory, is there anything else new recently?

M: Our Lady told me that I should tell the people that many in our time judge their faith by their priests. If a priest is not holy, they conclude that there is no God. She said: "You do not go to church to judge the priest, to examine his personal life. You go to church to pray and to hear the Word of God from the priest." This must be explained to the people, because many turn away from the faith because of priests.

In our time, the Virgin told me, God and the devil conversed, and the devil said that people believe in God only when life is good for them. When things turn bad, they cease to believe in God. Then people blame God, or act as if he does not exist.

God therefore, allowed the devil one century in which to exercise an extended power over the world, and the devil chose the twentieth century. Today, as we see all around us, everyone is dissatisfied; they cannot abide each other. Examples are the number of divorces and abortions. All this, Our Lady said, is the work of the devil.

T: You have said that the devil has entered into some marriages. Is his rule limited to those marriages?

M: No. That is just the beginning.

T: This behavior of people – they're under the influence of the devil. But the devil does not have to be in them?

M: No, no. The devil is not in them, but they're under the influence of the devil, although he enters into some of them.

To prevent this, at least to some extent, Our Lady said we need communal prayer, family prayer. She stressed the need for family prayer most of all. Also, every family should have at least one sacred object in the house, and houses should be blessed regularly.

She also emphasized the failings of religious people, especially in small villages – for example, here in Međugorje, where there is separation from Serbians (i.e., Serbian Orthodox) and Moslems. This separation is not good. Our Lady always stresses that there is but one God, and that people have enforced unnatural separation. One cannot truly believe, be a true Christian, if he does not respect other religions as well. You do not really believe in God if you make fun of other religions.

T: What, then, is the role of Jesus Christ, if the Moslem religion is a good religion?

M: We did not discuss that. She merely explained, and deplored, the lack of religious unity, "especially in the villages." She said that everybody's religion should be respected, and of course one's own.

T: Tell me where the devil is especially active today. Did she tell you anything about this? Through whom or what does he manifest himself most?

M: Most of all through people of weak character, who are divided within themselves Such people are everywhere, and they are the easiest for the devil to enter. But he also enters the lives of strong believers – sisters, for example. He would rather "convert" real believers than nonbelievers. How can I explain this? You saw what happened to me. He tries to bring as many believers as possible to himself.

T: What do you mean, "what happened to me"? Is that what you talked about before?

M: Yes.

T: You have never discussed what happened into my tape recorder. Please try to describe it now, so I can record it.

M: It was approximately six months ago, though I don't know exactly and cannot say for sure. As usual, I had locked myself into my room, alone, and waited for Our Lady. I knelt down, and had not yet made the sign of the cross, when suddenly a bright light flashed and a devil appeared. It was as if something had told me it was a devil. I looked at him and was very surprised, for I was expecting Our Lady to appear. He was horrible – he was like black all over and had a... He was terrifying, dreadful, and I did not know what he wanted. I realized I was growing weak, and then I fainted. When I revived, he was still standing there, laughing. It seemed that he gave me a strange kind of strength, so that I could almost accept him. He told me that I would be very beautiful, and very happy, and so on. However, I would have no need of Our Lady, he said, and no need for faith. "She has brought you nothing but suffering and difficulties," he said; but he would give me everything beautiful – whatever I want. Then something in me – I don't know what, if it was something conscious or something in my soul – told me: No! No! No! Then I began to shake and feel just awful. Then he disappeared, and Our Lady appeared, and when she appeared my strength returned – as if she had restored it to me. I felt normal again. Then Our Lady told me: "That was a trial, but it will not happen to you again."

T: Did Our Lady say anything else?

M: Nothing else. She told me it would not happen again and that she would talk to me about it later.

T: You said that the twentieth century has been given over to the devil?

M: Yes.

T: You mean the century until the year 2000, or generally speaking?

M: Generally, part of which is in the twentieth century, until the first secret is unfolded. The devil will rule till then. She told me several secrets and explained them to me; and I have written them down in code letters, with dates, so I won't forget them. If, say, tomorrow a secret is to be revealed, I have a right, two or three days before, to pick whatever priest I want and tell him about it. For example: "The day after tomorrow, such-and-such will happen." The priest, then, is free to do as he thinks best with that information. He can write it out before it happens, then read it to others after it happens. He can also tell it to the people: "Tomorrow, such-and-such will happen." It's up to him to decide what to do with the information."

T: Were these secrets ever revealed before, to anybody in previous generations?

M: I can't answer that.

T: Since you've been told not to talk about them, I won't ask you to. That's all right – as it should be. But I'll ask you if you know when the secrets will be revealed.

M: I know. I know every date of every secret.

T: But you can't say anything about this?

M: I can't.

T: Can we suppose, then, that one of you might say that three secrets would be revealed before the great sign appears; then the rest of the secrets will be revealed, one by one? Is there anything to that?

M: Nothing like that, but something like this. First, some secrets will be revealed – just a few. Then –. Then the people will be convinced that Our Lady was here. Then they will understand the sign. When Jakov said that the mayor will be the first one to run to the hill, he meant that generally, people of the highest social class. They will understand the sign as a place or occasion to convert. They will run to the hill and pray, and they will be forgiven. When I asked Our Lady about unbelievers, she said: "They should be prayed for, and they should pray." But when I asked again, recently, she said: "Let them convert while there is time." She did not say they should be prayed for.

T: You can say nothing specifically until the moment Our Lady says you can?

M: Yes.

T: Can we say that some secrets belong only to you, personally?

M: No. None of the secrets is personally for me.

T: Not you, then, but Ivan has received personal secrets.

M: My secrets are all for mankind generally, for the world, Međugorje, some other areas, and about the sign.

T: The sign will pertain to this parish?

M: Yes, to Međugorje. But there is something else.

T: Something else?

M: Nothing for me personally.

T: You have been given the last of the secrets?

M: Yes, the tenth.

T: Can you tell me what it relates to?

M: I cannot; but I can tell you that the eighth secret is worse than the other seven. I prayed for a long time that it might be less severe. Every day, when Our Lady came, I pestered her, asking that it be mitigated. Then she said that everyone should pray that it might be lessened. So, in Sarajevo, I got many people to join me in this prayer. Later, Our Lady told me that she'd been able to have the secret lessened. But then she told me the ninth secret and it was even worse. The tenth secret is totally bad and cannot be lessened whatsoever. I cannot say anything about it, because even a word would disclose the secret before it's time to do so.

T: I won't press you. Anyway, though, the tenth secret has to do with what will definitely happen?

M: Yes.

T: Unconditionally?

M: Yes. It will happen.

T: What does Our Lady say? Can we prepare ourselves for what will happen?

M: Yes, prepare! Our Lady said people should prepare themselves spiritually, be ready, and not panic; be reconciled in their souls. They should be ready for the worst, to die tomorrow. They should accept God now so that they will not be afraid. They should accept God, and everything else. No one accepts death easily, but they can be at peace in their souls if they are believers. If they are committed to God, he will accept them.

T: This means total conversion and surrender to God?

M: Yes.

T: After these ten secrets, after these eighteen months of apparitions, what do you tell the people they should do? What do you say to priests, to the Pope and bishops, without revealing the secrets? What does Our Lady want us to do?

M: First, I would like to tell you how it was for me at the end, and the...

T: All right.

M: Two days before Christmas, Our Lady told me Christmas Day would be the last time she would appear to me. (I didn't quite believe this.) On Christmas Day, she stayed with me for forty-five minutes and we talked about many things. We summarized everything that had been said between us. On behalf of many people, I asked what they should do. Then she gave me a very precious gift: she said she would appear to me on my birthday every year for the rest of my life. Also, independently of the sign – and anything else – she said she will appear to me when something very difficult happens – not some everyday difficulty, but something quite grievous. Then she will come to help me. But now, I have to live without her presence, without her daily, personal visits.

I say to all people: Convert! – the same as she said. "Convert while there is time!" Do not abandon God and your faith. Abandon everything else, but not that!

I ask priests to help their people, because priests can cause them to reject their faith. After a man has been ordained, he must really be a priest, bring people to the Church.

The most important point is that the people convert and pray.

T: What is the greatest danger to mankind? What does it come from?

M: From godlessness. Nobody believes – hardly anybody. For example, Our Lady told me that the faith in Germany, Switzerland, and Austria is very weak. The people in those countries model themselves on their priests, and if the priests are not good examples, the people fall away and believe there is no God. I heard of a priest to whom a rich man had left money to build a home for old people, but instead, the priest built a hotel. Now all the people in that city have turned their backs on the faith, because how could a priest not fulfill the last wish of a dying man and, instead, build a hotel and make money for himself? Nevertheless, people must understand that they shouldn't scrutinize a priest's private life, but listen to what he says through God – God's word.

T: Why did Our Lady introduce herself as the Queen of Peace?

M: You know very well that the situation of the world is horrible. There are wars in every part of the world. The situation is very tense. Peace is needed – a just and simple peace. First, peace in the soul; then...

T: So the message of Our Lady is a message of peace?

M: Yes. Primarily peace of the soul. If a person has it in his soul, he is surrounded by it.

T: Peace comes as a result of faith in God and surrender to him.

M: Yes; as a consequence of prayer, penance, and fasting.

T: Our Lady tells us that peace can be achieved that way; but evil things will happen nevertheless. Why?

M: They have to happen. The world has become very evil. It cares about faith very little. A while ago, I told you what she said when I decided to wear a cross around my neck. How many city people will say with approval: "What a sensible girl", and how many will say instead: "How stupid she is"?

T: I do not remember your saying that to me.

M: Our Lady was telling me at length how faith has declined. For example, now I live in the provincial capital, Sarajevo, and if I put a simple cross pendant around my neck and walked on the streets, how many people would say, or think to themselves "What a sensible girl!" and what proportion would say or think, "What a stupid or old-fashioned girl"? Nowadays, people curse God, Jesus Christ, his Mother, his Father, day in and day out, habitually. Besides, people have fallen into very evil ways, so that they live in evil routinely. It's no wonder that God is at the end of his patience.

T: Why do you think the Blessed Mother always exhorts the world, over and over again, to prayer and penance?

M: When we pray, we pray to God. (That's what you said in your sermon last night.) In return, we receive peace of soul, tranquility. We have opened our hearts to God, so that God can enter and when we have God in our heart and soul, we cannot cause evil to anybody. We will not curse – do anything evil. We will do good.

T: But Our Lady also says that we should pray for others.

M: We have to pray for anyone we see who is –. For example, I always pray for nonbelievers, because they do not know what is missing in their lives. They have no idea of how much they may have to suffer later. I pray that God will convert them, that he will give them a sign, that he will open their souls so that they can accept the faith.

T: I understand that, with prayer, we open ourselves to God, but Our Lady always seems to stress the need of prayer for others – prayer and fasting. Do you think that prayer and fasting bring a proper balance into the world? Do you feel that prayer and fasting can even partially atone for all the sins of the world?

M: Yes, I do; it's possible. Much can be done through prayer and fasting. Our Lady has said that prayer can stop wars and prevent catastrophes. Prayer and fasting! Of course prayer can help a struggling human who does not accept God and religion. Moreover, we are obliged to pray that such a person's heart will be opened. Again, I talk to many nonbelievers in Sarajevo and try to explain things to them so that they will gain at least a little understanding. Sometimes, it is not their fault; they received no religious training when they were young. Or later, when they abandoned their faith, no one tried to help them. I pray that God will open such hearts.

T: How do people react when you tell them such things? Do they accept you and what you say?

M: Well, it is usually in the classroom when I talk to people. They do not know that Our Lady has appeared to me. But they soon discover that I'm a believer, because when I hear somebody curse God, I ask them not to do it, at least not in front of me. Then they ask me if I believe, and I tell them I do. That way, we start a conversation, and I try to explain things: about God, who he is, and what he wants us to do. They seem to understand what I'm saying. Many, in fact, ask me to write out a prayer for them so they can say it at night. Really, they accept what I tell them. Only last night, I converted a grownup, a man. When you do something like that, convert somebody, you've introduced them to the faith, and you feel you've done something very important. A great feeling of peace comes into my soul, a special joy. Somehow, your whole soul starts to glitter.

J: Have you received any special messages for priests and bishops?

M: No; but a long time ago, she said that they should accept us, help us as much as they can, and pray more and do penance.

T: Priests and bishops, too?

M: Yes.

T: So you were given no special message for any priest?

M: No. Not exactly.

T: For the Pope?

M: No. I never even asked about the Pope.

T: You didn't ask?

M: No.

T: And Our Lady didn't say anything about the Pope?

M: Nothing.

T: Did she ever mention the "Case of Herzegovina," the situation here?

M: No, she didn't.

T: She did not; but did you ask her any questions about it?

M: I did not, except the time you told me to ask.

T: Can you deduce anything about it from your conversations with her?

M: I don't know what to say. Maybe I can tell you about when she stopped appearing to me.

T: Yes?

M: I asked her why, why I had to be the first. She said that she had stayed with us a long time, longer than is necessary, but that this is the last apparition on earth...

T: What do you mean, "the last apparition on earth"?

M: It is the last time that Jesus or Mary will appear on earth.

T: What do you mean, "appear"?

M: The last time they will appear, so that you can speak with them.

T: You mean that this is the last apparition in this era, in this period of the Church, or that they will never again come to earth?

M: I don't know. Our Lady said this is the last apparition on earth. I cannot understand exactly what this means.

T: I once asked the other visionaries if this is the last apparition in this period of Church history, or whether it means the end of the world or that Mary will never appear again. They told me she said "in this period."

M: I don't know. She said she will not appear on earth. I do not know if she means this era. I do not know how to ask such a question properly.

T: Did you ever ask about other apparitions in the world – Our Lady's apparitions in our time at other places?

M: She mentioned a man in Germany who caused panic among the people – on buses, trains, and the like – telling them: "Convert! While there is yet time!" There are many false prophets in our time, she said, throughout the world, who lie, claiming to see Our Lady or Jesus. This is a great sin, and we should pray for such people. In fact, she and I prayed for fourteen days, exclusively, for false prophets. They do not understand how grave a sin it is to lie about having visions.

Anyway, I asked her why she would no longer appear to me, after such a long time, and she explained that because I had decided to continue my school, I must learn to live my life without her direct help and advice. She told me that I'm no different from any other young person, any other girl, and that I must live accordingly – although she will visit me on every birthday. Till then, I may think about all sorts of questions to ask her and what I would like her to do for me.

T: She said because you decided to continue your schooling. If you had decided to enter a convent and live the life of a religious, would she continue to appear? What do you think?

M: I think she would, but I'm not sure. But maybe she wouldn't! She has already stayed on earth too long, she said, and hadn't intended to stay even this length of time. So I can't say what she would do if I went into a convent instead of continuing school. Anyway, she promised me this marvelous gift on my birthdays.

T: Before we finish this interview, is there anything you would like to add?

M: She said some things that are for me personally. She advised me on various matters. Then she said: "Go in God's peace!"

T: Did she talk to you about the other visionaries and further apparitions?

M: She told me I am – well, more mature than the others and therefore I must help them, spend time with them and talk with them. This will make things easier for them and me. We are to understand each other and stay together – united.

T: She did not mention further developments or apparitions, either individually or to all of you as a group?

M: I think that when each individual learns the tenth secret, she will cease appearing to that person.

T: You don't know if she has future plans for you or any
of the group?

M: I don't think she does, because she said...

(End of tape, side 1)

T: Tell me, Mirjana, how did you feel after your last
meeting with Our Lady?

M: After she left, I just sat there, like a statue. I felt very
strange. I thought to myself: "This can't be true; she
will come again. I will pray at the same times, and she
will return." I was very restless and I insisted on being
alone. I locked myself into my room and thought: "She
will come again; she will not come again." I didn't
know what to think, what to do. How can I live without her? What will happen to me? Then I would pray,
long and hard, as if I were in a trance. I would ask myself: "Why has this happened? Why is she not here?
She will not come again." Oh, it was terrible, terrible!

T: You were very depressed?

M: What do you' mean, "depressed"?

T: Well, sad.

M: Terribly sad. At school, everybody told me I'd gone
mad. They laughed at me. I didn't want to talk to anybody. Before, I wouldn't let on to anybody that I was
suffering; but now, for about the last fourteen days,
since this has happened, I've just wanted to sit by myself, alone. In the classroom, I didn't know what was
happening. If a professor calls on me, I'm unable to
answer. If he asks why I don't listen, why I do the
things I do, I start to cry, without knowing why. I was

terribly sensitive, and my life has been really terrible. Now, little by little, life is easier; but it is still very difficult.

T: You were thinking about Our Lady all that time?

M: Oh, yes! I smile; then immediately I think: "If I smile, she will not come." So I become my old self again – sad. I always become sad when I remind myself that she will not come. The sadness comes all by itself, it seems, and there is a terrible pain in my soul.

T: Can you, nevertheless – in your prayers, in your inner self – feel some sense of her presence?

M: Yes, I can! I felt her last night, when we prayed the seven Our Fathers. The feeling was beautiful, as if I were praying with her. It was as if I heard her voice in my heart, echoing in me and praying together with me. I was aware of nothing around me. I simply immersed myself in praying, as she does. I heard our two voices echoing.

T: Did you really hear her voice, or did it just seem that you heard her?

M: I can't say for sure. When I prayed, I heard her voice, as I told you. Even though I was completely immersed in prayer, I heard her, her resonant voice. It was exactly as if she was praying with me. It was beautiful. I was praying Our Father from the beginning, not just the second half (the response). I prayed the other prayers, too, and it was exactly as if she was with me.

T: Did you hear her voice in yours ears, or – somehow – in your heart?

M: In my soul.

T: What is your habit of praying now, and do you have favorite prayers?

M: Now, since Our Lady has ceased appearing to me, and if my school classes are in the morning, I go into my room in the afternoon, at the time that she used to appear. I pray the rosary and I pray for an hour or two, depending on how much time I have. But usually never less than one hour. I pray that God will give me the strength of soul that I can again think and behave normally. I also pray for unbelievers, for their conversion. And for the secrets.

T: Do you like to read Holy Scripture?

M: I have a Bible, an old copy, but I don't have the Holy Scripture.

T: They're the same thing.

M: That is the same? I didn't know they mean the same thing.

T: I meant the Gospels. 1 wanted to ask if you read them.

M: Oh, yes. There are many beautiful things and sayings in them.

T: Do you read the Gospels regularly? Has anybody instructed you in how to read them, or do you read on your own?

M: I haven't consulted anybody about this. When I pray, something comes to me, because I immerse myself in prayer. Then it's as if I'm speaking with someone. I express things the way I think they should be said, all the while talking to God. Then I go back to saying the regular kind of prayers. Then I pray again in my own words. I say all this out loud.

T: Is anybody with you when you pray? Is there a prayer group or do you get together...?

M: Mostly I'm alone. My mother works, but sometimes she joins me when she is home. And sister Marinka. Sometimes we pray together.

T: Do you remember any other important details from your conversations? Do any other details come to mind, from the times you talked with Our Lady?

M: I can't remember any.

T: Do you know of any healing that's connected with you?

M: Yes, in Sarajevo. A man wrote to me to thank me.

T: What happened?

M: I had all that in Sarajevo. I wrote it all down in my notebook. He was in a wheelchair, unable to walk, and he wrote me a very beautiful letter, full of strong emotions, telling me about his suffering. I asked Our Lady to help him, and she told me that he is a firm believer but that he should pray more. He prays, but not for himself. And he should pray for himself, that he might be healed. Anyway, he finally prayed, and I prayed, and after three months he wrote to me again and said he could walk a little. He can get on his feet and walk a little with one crutch. He wrote to thank me.

T: So Our Lady said that if we pray for a particular need...

M: We should emphasize exactly that: Dear God, I'm praying to be healed of my illness. Pray like that. But pray from your heart, from the bottom of your soul, with feeling. It does not have to be a "regular" prayer, but a conversation with God. "God, you see my suffering. You know how I am. I'm not complaining, my cross is not too difficult to bear; but I would like to be on my feet again so I can move around in the world." Like that: conversation, then prayer.

T: How long should we pray?

M: I believe that sick people should speak and pray to God for one hour every day, intimately. I'm sure it would restore their souls and that God would grant them grace.

T: Did Our Lady ever recommend special devotions?

M: She always recommended faith, prayer, and penance. She never mentioned anything special for anybody, whether they were sick or healthy. But, as I told you, she said we should direct our prayers: "I am praying for such-and-such." And we should pray with concentration, not race through the words of Our Father. The main thing is not to say the words of a prayer, but to feel them.

T: And fasting?

M: She said that sick people do not have to fast. If they do not fast, it is not a sin for them. They can do another good deed instead. For those who are able to fast, it is not enough that they do a good deed instead.

T: Does she say fasting must be on bread and water only, or are other kinds of fasting acceptable?

M: We did not discuss fasting except on bread and water. But probably she meant we should fast only on bread and water.

T: Everybody?

M: Yes – everybody who wants to receive something from God or have God's help.

T: Are there any other points you want to mention?

M: Not that I can remember.

This conversation was held with Mirjana after Our Lady ceased to appear to her, December 25, 1982.

XV

INTERVIEW WITH IVANKA IVANKOVIĆ

By Fr. Svetozar Kraljević
Međugorje, February 27, 1983

Fr. S: Ivanka, you and Mirjana were taking a walk together that day. Why were you walking together?

I: We regularly walked together in that area. We had been at my house; then we decided to take our walk.

S: Who was with you, besides Mirjana?

I: At first, just Mirjana and myself. When we returned to my house, Milka, Marija's sister, asked us to go with her to get the sheep and bring them home.

S: So the two of you went with Milka to get the sheep?

I: The first time, Mirjana and I were walking alone, and as we were returning to the village I happened to look toward the hill – and I saw the figure of Our Lady, bright and shining. I said to Mirjana: "Look, Our Lady!" Mirjana dismissed what I said with a wave of her hand, as if I'd been joking, and said: "It's not very likely that Our Lady would appear to us." So we continued to walk toward the village. Mirjana did not even look where I pointed to the hill. When we got to Milka's house, Milka said: "Help me get the sheep and bring them home." So we turned around and started walking back to the fields. This time, all three of us saw Our Lady. We knelt down and prayed; then we got the sheep and chased them home. Later, Vicka and Ivan and the other Ivan joined us.

S: On that first day, you saw Our Lady twice?

I: Yes. The first time when Mirjana and I were walking back to the village, and the second time when we went with Milka to get the sheep.

S: Who saw Our Lady first?

I: I did.

S: What did you say when you saw her?

I: I said: "Look, Mirjana, Our Lady!"

S: What was in your mind that made you say, "Look, Our Lady!"?

I: I saw her outline, the same as I'd seen in holy pictures. That's all I can say – I can't describe it better.

S: When you said, "Look, Our Lady!" did you say it more to yourself or more to Mirjana?

I: To myself and Mirjana; but probably more to myself.

S: Then what did you do? Where did you go?

I: We went to Milka's. We stopped in front of her house and she asked us to help her get the sheep. Then the three of us went to get the sheep to bring them home. When we passed the hill, I saw Our Lady again, this time holding the Baby Jesus in her hands. Mirjana and Milka also looked and they, too, saw Our Lady.

S: What did seeing Our Lady mean to you?

I: It meant everything in the world!

S: My impression is that it didn't mean very much to you the first time you saw her, because you said, "Look, Our Lady!" but kept walking.

I: I didn't believe I saw what I thought I was seeing. I was confused by it all. I couldn't tell what had happened, whether I was having a hallucination of some kind. But the second time I was sure.

S: The second time, while you were looking at the hill, Vicka joined you?

I: Yes, and she asked what we were looking at. She thought we were looking at a snake. We said, "Our Lady" but she took her shoes off and ran away. Then Ivan and the other Ivan came, and Vicka came back with them, and they looked at Our Lady with us.

S: This time, did you believe what you thought you saw before your eyes?

I: I did, and I was shaking. I don't know what the others saw or believed.

S: What do you mean, "shaking"?

I: The first time, I was afraid. We were all afraid. How would you feel if something like that happened to you?

S: Ivanka, try to list all the places where Our Lady has appeared to you.

I: On the hill, in several houses, in the village, in the fields, in the rectory, in Cerno, and in the church.

S: When you talk with Our Lady in your visions, we cannot hear you speak.

I: We speak out loud, the same as now.

S: Let me put it this way. Do you speak with Our Lady mentally – that is, she understands what you think – or do you speak to her in a low voice, a whisper, so we cannot hear you? Or is your conversation miraculous – beyond our power to hear and understand?

I: I speak with her normally, the same as I'm speaking now. Also, I hear her voice and words in the normal way, as well as what the others say.

S: You, know, Ivanka, that all this is beyond my understanding.

I: What can I do! God's power!

S: When you speak, can you feel the movement here in your throat?

I: Just as now – the same way.

S: Must we believe, then, that your visions are miraculous, especially as we hear not a word of what you say? Do you believe it's a miracle?

I: I believe it is.

S: In your visions, have you ever asked favors for anybody?

I: I have. In the beginning, I asked a favor for little Daniel.

S: What did Our Lady say?

I: She said the same thing she always says: that strong faith and prayer will help.

S: What do you mean, "strong faith and prayer"? For what?

I: To believe and pray for a healing.

S: Did you ever ask about anybody in your family?

I: Yes. I asked about my father not long ago, and she said the same thing.

S: Did you ever ask about anybody in your family who has passed away?

I: Yes. I asked about my mother on the second day.

S: What did Our Lady say?

I: She said my mother is with her, and that I should obey and not worry.

S: You were saddened by your mother's death, and because of that Our Lady came to comfort you.

I: I don't know, but I don't think so. We asked her why, of all people, she appeared to us. She said she does not always seek out the best people.

S: What does Our Lady's appearance mean for the world?

I: I think it means something momentous.

S: To whom are Our Lady's messages sent?

I: To the whole world.

S: What are the messages?

I: Peace, conversion, fasting, penance, prayer.

S: Which is the most important?

I: Peace.

S: Why peace?

I: When everyone in the world is at peace, everything is possible.

S: Can you tell us something about this peace? What did Our Lady say about it?

I: I think that peace is most important.

S: Do you intend to direct your life in such a way as to achieve peace in the world?

I: As much as it is in my power.

S: You mentioned prayer. Tell me honestly, how do you pray?

I: When I get up in the morning, I pray seven Our Fathers and the Credo. At noon, I pray the Angelus. In the evening, I pray seven Our Fathers and the Credo, and sometimes the rosary. When we are all home together, we pray an evening prayer.

S: How often do you go to church?

I: I go to church regularly, and when I come here to Međugorje.

S: It is known that Our Lady recommended that all of you enter a convent.

I: She told us it is her wish that we enter a convent – but only those who have such a wish. She does not want anyone to disgrace the faith and the Church.

S: I believe that everyone is free to choose, and you are free as well. Have you decided what you will do in this connection?

I: To tell you the truth, as I feel right now, I do not want to enter the convent. I can live a Christian life, the same as a nun, raising... That is my opinion.

S: When you went to a specialist in Mostar for an examination, what did they tell you?

I: They attacked and libeled us.

S: Who did?

I: The lady doctor, Džudža.

S: What did she say?

I: She said we had made it all up.

5: Did they question you?

I: We went there, among people who are mentally ill, they questioned us. Then we left.

S: How long did you stay in Mostar?

I: We arrived at eight in the morning and left at one in the afternoon.

S: What is the reason for Our Lady's appearances?

I: I think because the world is going in a wrong direction, and she came to reconcile the world.

S: What is Our Lady's name?

I: The Queen of Peace.

S: "The Queen of Peace." Does she mean to imply something by that name?

I: I think that, in calling herself Queen of Peace, she shows that she means to reconcile the world.

S: How does she reconcile the world?

I: Merely by coming to the world, she reconciles it – at least a little. People have converted, and begun to believe, and pray a little more. Our Lady said that with prayer and fasting wars could be stopped.

S: Bearing in mind what you know about the future, tell me if Our Lady of Međugorje will reconcile the world even more.

I: I think she will. Because she is the Queen of Peace, I think she will reconcile the whole world.

S: Will the "great sign" help in achieving this?

I: Yes, when the time comes. More believers will come to church.

S: Will the sign appear very soon, or later?

I: It will appear at the proper time.

S: Ivanka, are you in any way fearful of being able to do what Our Lady expects of you in this life?

I: Why should I be afraid when God is with me? God gives me whatever strength I need.

S: You speak to the people of Our Lady's messages, but some do not believe you. In that case, what do you do?

I: I pray for them, that God will enlighten them.

S: Can you do anything else?

I: I will go on trying to persuade them. They will be convinced, once they...

S: I believe that, but in the meantime people become nervous. It is difficult to wait for that day. What should people do?

I: Pray that God will give us the strength to endure.

S: There are those who are opposed to Our Lady. What would you tell them?

I: I'd tell them: Convert! There is a God. That is it!

S: Can those who oppose Our Lady frustrate her plans in the world?

I: You mean the great sign?

S: Yes.

I: No. All their armaments and explosives could not destroy it.

S: Can they do harm to the souls of the people and to Our Lady's plans for the people?

I: No.

S: Does that mean Our Lady is stronger than they?

I: Normally she is. It is Jesus who decides – God. Not Our Lady.

S: Tell me about that.

I: I think that God has sent her here. When we asked her for a sign, I think she asked Jesus and he gave her a sign. Then she promised to give us a sign.

S: That means she cannot act independently, on her own. She must do the will of God, as she always has.

I: I believe so.

S: Do you believe she wishes her voice to be heard throughout the world?

I: I think she wants to reconcile the entire world.

S: What does she talk to you about now?

I: Her life.

S: Can you tell me anything about it?

I: No. When she is finished, we will give the account to whomever she tells us.

S: Did she tell you not to speak about it and not give the account to a priest?

I: She did; and we do what she tells us.

S: Mirjana's grandmother once told you to pray seven Our Fathers, which may mean that this directive is not necessarily a directive of Our Lady.

I: It wasn't – at the beginning. But then we asked her what prayers she likes most, and she said she likes the Creed, the song "Kriste, u tvoje ime" and seven Our Fathers.

S: So you were praying on your own initiative at first, until later she approved what you'd been praying and told you to continue?

I: Yes.

S: From what you know, what do people ask for most: healing of the body or the soul?

I: Most people ask for a healing of the soul, because the soul is more important. Today we live on earth, but tomorrow we must leave this earth.

S: What would you say to people you will never see, never meet, although they will read your words and the message of Our Lady?

I: Keep the faith; persevere in it. Help your friends. Do not be snobbish toward other religions, but respect them insofar as they praise God.

S: It is important that people of good faith, regardless of denomination, not be turned against each other. But tell me more about this. What did Our Lady say about this?

I: Our Lady said that religions are separated in the earth, but the people of all religions are accepted by her Son.

S: Does that mean that all people go to Heaven?

I: It depends on what they deserve.

S: Yes, but many have never heard about Jesus.

I: Jesus knows all about that; I don't. Our Lady said, basically, religions are similar; but many people have separated themselves, because of religion and become enemies of each other.

S: I thank you, Ivanka, for this conversation and testimony!

XVI

INTERVIEW WITH MARINKO AND DRAGICA IVANKOVIĆ

By Fr. Svetozar Kraljević
Međugorje, February 27, 1983

Marinko Ivanković was born in 1943 in Bijakovići, Međugorje, where he lives.

Marija Pavlović was the first person who told him about the apparitions of the Blessed Virgin Mary, on the morning of June 25, when he took her and Vicka Ivanković to Čitluk for summer-school classes. In the afternoon of the same day, he sought out Ivan Dragičević, who also saw the apparition, to learn more about what had happened. He agreed to visit the site of the apparition, but he arrived there late. (He mistakenly believed the time of the apparition was 7:15 p.m., not 6:15.) On the third day, he became a coordinator and supporter of the group of visionaries, and has been associated with them ever since. He has been with them at all important moments – joy, prayer, revelation – and also at the moments of sufferings and persecution. The following is a transcript of our conversation.

S: Marinko, what's brought you into such close contact with the group of visionaries? Why have you involved yourself so closely with them?

M: I'll tell you. I attend "marriage weekends" and am a practicing believer. Also, the children have sometimes found themselves in difficult circumstances, especially Ivanka. She was the first in the group who saw the light and Our Lady. Her mother was dead and her father was in Germany. Practically, too, Jakov does not have a father; he lives in Bosnia but rarely visits here. Then Mirjana's family lives in Sarajevo. In one way or another, the children did not have parental advice or the protection of parents. So I got to know them with only one thought in mind: to give them strength, in place of their parents. "Backup," you might say. I wanted to preserve their morale and thereby help them.

S: So you thought they needed help?

M: Right. Someone had to help them, protect them. They had to know that someone is on their side, that they're not alone. Later, I knew that I'd really helped, because they believed me more than anyone else.

S: More than the priests?

M: Absolutely more than the priests, who didn't go there. Absolutely.

S: Were you the first person who told the priests?

M: Yes, I was. On the second day, I was late, and when I got there I saw the children coming down the hill from where they'd seen the vision. Ivanka was coming down the hill and her grandmother was waiting for her on the road. Ivanka was crying. Then Ivanka embraced her grandmother and said: "Grandma, I asked Our Lady about my mother, and she said mother is well and in Heaven." I tried to calm her down, but I couldn't. She kept on crying. Then I decided to go to the priests to tell them what had happened, because it was something out of this world. I thought someone should try to help, someone who knew more about such things than I did – especially a priest, because it's connected with the faith. So the priests should be told about it. Especially, because this might not be true, they should investigate and warn the people.

So I went to the rectory. Two nuns were standing on the stairs at the front door of the rectory, and I asked them if a priest was home. "Zrinko," one of them said, and I thought to myself: "I prefer Fr. Jozo; it would be easier to talk to him." Anyway, Zrinko came to the door and said: "How are you, Marinko? What's new?" We greeted each other; then I told him: "Father, I came to tell you that last night and this evening, some children have been saying they've seen the Blessed Virgin Mary, Our Lady. Now they're crying and troubled. I think you should see them and try to console them – talk to them and find out if what they've been saying is true." Then Fr. Zrinko said: "Marinko, let those who have been allowed to see it, see it; and those who have not been allowed, not see it."

So I went back home. But everyone in the village was talking about the children's visions.

S: What did you think about what he said?

M: I didn't think he was right, but who was I to argue with him? I felt let down, discouraged. I wanted him to go with me to see the children and talk with them – to see for himself. Maybe we would have found out something important. I couldn't understand why he wouldn't go with me. He acted as if he couldn't care less if Our Lady had appeared. I couldn't understand – it didn't seem possible.

S: Dragica (Marinko's wife), I understand that you were the first one who informed Fr. Jozo, the pastor, about the apparitions. What happened?

D: I was working on Saturday (June 27) and a heavy piece of metal fell on my hand and also broke my leg. So they took me to the hospital in Mostar and when we got to the front of the hospital, Fr. Jozo was there visiting his mother. He saw me and asked what had happened. "Nothing serious," I said; "but where have you been? You should be in Međugorje! Our Lady's appeared!" He asked me who'd told me that and I said: "The children – five or six of them – who've seen Our Lady for the last two evenings! Zrinko doesn't seem to believe it; so you should go and see for yourself!"

S: This brings up an interesting point. Providentially, God called on the two of you to inform the priests – the Church. You, Marinko, went to the rectory and you, Dragica, were injured so that you had to be taken to the hospital, where you saw Fr. Jozo, who was visiting his sick mother. Moreover, Marinko, you've had several unusual experiences. Tell me about them.

M: Yes, I have – several. One evening, about twenty days after the first apparition, Our Lady told the children to go to the hill later in the evening, about 11:00, to the place where she'd appeared. Then the children invited me to go with them, me and some other believers from the village, about thirty or forty all together. As soon as we got there, we started to pray. Then I looked up and it seemed that the sky had opened with a very bright light, maybe fifteen feet across, and something was coming toward us. Everyone saw it and said at the same time: "Look! See the bright light!"

We were standing in a circle around the hole where the people had dug up the ground and taken the soil home with them, when Our Lady appeared. There was a wooden cross in the hole, and it seemed as if a large globe of light was bursting from the cross into thousands of bright stars. The light was too bright for me to look at, while all this was happening, so I can't tell you exactly what happened. Later, we talked this over among ourselves, and no one else can say exactly what happened.

Some of the children were scared and began to scream; so I wanted to quiet them down. As soon as I began to try, Marija said: "Be calm. Our Lady is with us!" Then, for the next forty minutes, we knelt and prayed together. We were crying, too! I'll never forget that experience! It was a different kind of prayer, and you know that God is with you – and Jesus and Our Lady. After forty minutes, everybody stood up and the children told us: "Our Lady is looking at all of you and says that you may touch her." So we all rushed to the spot where we thought Our Lady was standing. As the children led us to the exact spot, someone stepped on her veil and at that point the children said: "She's gone away."

However, some of those who had touched her said their hands seemed to go numb. Meanwhile, people from the neighborhood of Čilići had seen a circle of light around the spot where Our Lady had been, and some of them were climbing the hill at the same time that we were trying to touch Our Lady. After Our Lady left, we all returned home together.

S: Have you experienced anything like that, before or since?

M: I have. Jakov and Vicka invited me to go with them when they were supposed to have a vision in Vicka's house, in her bedroom. I was making grape brandy, as I always do at that time of year, and some children were singing religious songs. Jakov asked me to go with him, and I did – with my son, Davor, and another child, Matan Šego. As we were going up the steps of Vicka's house, Jakov said: "Marinko, Our Lady is here!"

This was exactly two days before Fr. Jozo's trial. I ran up the steps, then knelt at the door, and my son and Matan knelt behind me. I stretched out my hands and said: "Dear Our Lady! Prove to the unbelievers that Fr. Jozo is innocent." I paid no attention to what Jakov and Vicka were doing, though they were speaking to Our Lady, until they said to me: "Marinko, Our Lady is smiling at you and moving toward you." "She's kissing, embracing, and blessing you," they told me. At first, I felt nothing; nothing at all, then, I felt as if my heart would break out of my chest. It was a feeling of great excitement.

"Our Lady is telling you," they told me, "to cling to your faith; do not abandon it." Then I said: "I am not afraid to give my life for Jesus, if he will show me what I must do."

Then Jakov and Vicka repeated Our Lady's words: "These beautiful children are glorifying me!" She must have meant the two children who were with me, who had been singing religious songs. Other children had followed us and were singing hymns in the street, and Jakov and Vicka said that Our Lady wanted all of them brought to her so she could bless them. The children went up the stairs, my mother and sister-in-law were also there, near the door. Then Jakov and Vicka turned and said: "Our Lady is above you, blessing everyone." That was the end of the apparition that night.

S: Tell me, Marinko, about the vision in the field.

M: It happened here in the field one evening, after the children had returned from Mass in the church and after the prayers for the sick. The people from the neighborhood, as usual, had gathered in the field between Međugorje and Čilići. Later, as this became known beyond the neighborhood, more and more people joined us. Some were merely curious and some were secret police. But I don't know this for sure. Anyway, who cares?

We prayed and sang there, and one evening, on the Feast of Our Lady of the Angels, the six visionaries joined us in prayer and Our Lady appeared to them. All together, we prayed the seven Our Fathers, Hail Marys, Glorias, and the Credo. Then the children told us: "Our Lady will allow all who wish to go to her and touch her." As they led the people to her, one by one, they'd say: "Now you are touching her veil, her head, her hand, her dress." This went on for ten or fifteen minutes, until Our Lady departed. Just then, Marija cried out and I ran to her.

"What's wrong, Marija?" I asked. "Oh, Marinko," she said, "Our Lady is blackened all over!" "Why was she blackened all over?" I asked. "There were sinners here who touched her," Marija said, "and as they touched her, her robe got darker and darker, until it was black." Then she said that everyone should go to confession as soon as possible, but I stayed a little longer to talk to her.

She told me that when she'd been alone, in her room, she'd had a vision of Our Lady – that evening, after she returned from church, as she was changing clothes to go to the field. "This evening," she said, "the Virgin told me everything! 'The devil is trying to insert himself into all this, at whatever price. He'll try anything; but my Son wants to win over all souls for himself. Even so, the devil is striving to win every soul he can. He's making every effort, paying any price, to insert himself among you.'"

Dragica and Marinko Ivanković, July 2005

XVII

TESTIMONY OF FR. LUKA SUŠAC

Fr. Luka was born on the Feast of St. Francis of Assisi – October 4, 1922. He attended school in Ljubuški and Široki Brijeg. He completed his theological studies in Zagreb, where he was ordained in 1947.

He served as associate pastor in Mostar for two years, as pastor in Konjic for four years, as guardian and pastor of the monastery of Široki Brijeg for two years, as guardian and pastor of the monastery of Humac for six years, as pastor in Vitina for ten years, and as pastor in Međugorje for six years. Today, Fr. Luka is a member of a pastoral team in the major Franciscan parish and monastery of Humac.

Regularly, every day, four Franciscan priests from the monastery of Humac – Frs. Janko Bubalo, Vinko Dragičević, Stanko Vasilj, and I – go to Međugorje to help hear confessions. October 22, 1981, was no different from any other day, until late afternoon.

We arrived at Međugorje about 4:15, and I had just parked the car in front of the parish rectory when Fr. Zrinko Čuvalo, the acting pastor, asked me to stay at the parish office before we began to hear confessions. Many people had been stopping at the office to talk with the local priests, and Fr. Čuvalo asked me to help out because I had been pastor of the parish for more than six years (previous to the apparitions of Our Lady) and knew the parishioners and, presumably, was familiar with many local problems.

I went into the office, to await the expected parishioners, and in an idle moment glanced through a window toward the hill of Križevac. I noticed, instead of a cross, what seemed to be a white pillar of bright light, which soon took on the contour or outline of a woman. I immediately called for Fr. Tomislav Vlašić to come to the office and look through the window. "Look toward Križevac!" I almost shouted. He looked for a moment, then left the room and returned with a pair of binoculars, with which we examined the unusual light. Then Frs. Janko and Stanko came to the window and the four of us took turns looking through the binoculars. I had two turns with the binoculars.

Looking through the window with the binoculars, I saw what seemed to be a statue of a woman with her arms extended, looking toward the parish church. Rather than "statue" perhaps I should say "outline," for I could not make out the eyes, or mouth, or hair. At times, it seemed, the figure bowed to her left, then to her right. The figure was visible for approximately half an hour.

It would be inaccurate to say simply that I was excited; throughout my body coursed a sensation of joy – an awareness of joy – or maybe pure joy itself. I remember a thought that passed through my mind: "This is a reward from Our Lady for our exhausting four months of hearing confessions in Međugorje."

Many pilgrims, in and outside the church, also saw this unusual appearance. Those who had been inside the church came out on the lawn, and everybody was kneeling, praying, singing, and uttering gasps of joy. All heads were turned toward Križevac and all faces were bright with exultation.

I am willing to confirm the truthfulness of this testimony by oath at any time!

(signed) Fr. Luka Sušac

Father Luka died September 21, 1997, as he was dressing himself to celebrate Holy Mass.

XVIII

TESTIMONY OF
FR. UMBERTO LONČAR

Fr. Lončar, a highly valued and well-thought-of Franciscan priest in the Province of Herzegovina, was born in Posušje on June 6, 1922, where he attended primary school. He joined the Franciscans in 1940 and completed his theological studies in Zagreb, where he was ordained a priest June 6, 1949 (his twenty-seventh birthday). Thereupon he spent a year in military service, after which he was assigned to Mostar and then to Konjic as associate pastor. He remained in Konjic till 1952, when he became pastor in Crnač. He was pastor in Čerin from 1959 to 1964, pastor in Humac from 1964 to 1970, and pastor in Posuški Gradac from 1970 to 1978, when he was sent to Gradniće. In 1988 he came to Čerin where he is now. At Humac, he was also guardian of the monastery from 1967 until he was assigned to Posuški Gradac.

On August 2 and 3, 1981 (Sunday and Monday), many pilgrims in Međugorje saw that the sun had grown dim and was orbited by bright rings that cast reddish rays upon the church at Međugorje. Later, bright circles of various colors rotated around the sun. This was seen by pilgrims during Our Lady's appearance to the children, from about 6:20 to 6:40 p.m., and of course produced unusual talk and speculation as word of these occurrences spread far and near.

On Sunday, I had noticed nothing at all of this, and did not believe that any of it happened. However, I must admit, I had not observed the sun or the sky by even the most casual glance.

Monday, because of the reports about the Sunday happenings, I made it a point to observe the sun and the sky – and saw the same phenomena repeated. The sky in the other direction – that is, north of the church – was traversed by an arc of dark globes, moving from east to west. I tried to dismiss all this as unusual but natural phenomena, produced by weather and/or temperature abnormalities. Or perhaps my looking into the sun had caused these unreal images. In short, none of this, I told myself, was miraculous.

The next day, however (Tuesday, Aug. 4), I had what I must call a "special vision." Purposely, I had stayed home, and did not go to Međugorje. When I left the house, at 6:00 p.m., I spread a hand before my face and, through slits between my fingers, glanced at the sun, whose light was fading. A light breeze had arisen and the early evening was very pleasant. After I glanced at the sun, I looked away, in the direction of Međugorje, because I did not want my vision to be affected by direct observation of the sun. I did not see any "dark globes," but exactly at 6:20 I saw a huge red and violet cloud over Cerno. The cloud was massive and was moving in my direction at unusual – tremendous – speed, then hovered over the hill of Križevac for one or two minutes, moved eastward, and seemed to sink to the earth. Because of the hills and trees between me and the cloud, I couldn't see what happened; so I ran to the upper floor of the rectory to have a better view. After the cloud disappeared from sight, I descended to the terrace between the rectory and the church. Precisely at 6:40, the red and violet figure of a magnificent lady arose from the hill of Crnica. The red and violet faded in intensity as she ascended in the sky; then she disappeared. The last thing I saw was a brilliant white scarf that dangled from her feet and swung in the air.

The vision of the lady ascending into the sky lasted about 30 seconds.

This experience, I have no doubt, was supernatural. Therefore, it is a proof that the events in Međugorje originate with God.

I have given this much thought, and the following points (among many others) seem especially obvious and pertinent.

1. The skies on that early Tuesday evening were clear and absolutely cloudless – although I did not look toward the sun, so that my vision would not be affected. However, I have never seen a cloud, before or since, like the cloud that suddenly appeared over Cerno.
2. The figure that appeared in the sky was of a beautiful woman, which I saw sharply and clearly – unmistakably – and whom I must say was Our Lady.
3. The scarf or veil that dangled beneath her feet was whiter than the whitest snow.
4. The figure was that of a high-born woman.
5. Reason disallows mere coincidence and sensory vagaries. At the exact same time I saw what I have described above, Our Lady appeared to the children in a garden in Bijakovići.

I must conclude that I witnessed a miraculous sign: our heavenly Mother, whom the children see and talk with.

PART 4
MISSION OF MEĐUGORJE FRIENDS

XIX

THE MISSION AND RESPONSIBILITY
OF THE FRIENDS OF MEÐUGORJE

I shall begin with the title and shall try to clarify how I understood it, and in which direction it leads us.

The mission of the faithful can only be the biblical mission, which is the same for human beings from the very beginning: the mission given to Adam and Eve in the Book of Genesis, the mission of men in the New Testament, the mission of Mary, the mission given to the apostles, the mission in which the Church was born. The mission can exist only within the framework of the Church and never outside of the frame given by Christ when he had chosen and sent out his disciples. Nothing can change in it, neither in time nor in space. The mission and responsibility in Meðugorje can henceforth not be different. Our mission and our responsibility are rooted in human nature, illuminated by a divine light through the Revelation.

The first page of the Catechism of the Catholic Church begins with a number of fundamental biblical texts, which I shall take here as a basis that carries everything, including what Meðugorje may mean in the Church. "FATHER, ... this is eternal life, that they may know you, the only true God, and Jesus Christ whom you have sent." (Jn 17:3) "God our Savior desires all men to be saved and to come to the knowledge of the truth" (1 Tim 2:3-4) because "There is no other name under heaven given among men by which we must be saved" (Ac 4:12) than the name of JESUS.

The Catechism of the Catholic Church continues: "So that this call should resound throughout the world, Christ sent forth the apostles he had chosen, commissioning them to proclaim the gospel: "Go therefore and make disciples of all nations, baptizing them in the name of the Father and of the Son and of the Holy Spirit, teaching them to observe all that I have commanded you; and lo, I am with you always, to the end of the age." (Mt 28:19-20) Strengthened by this mission, the apostles "went forth and preached everywhere, while the Lord worked with them and confirmed the message by the signs that attended it." (Mk 16:20)

The mission and responsibility of Christians of our times derive from the same roots as the mission and the responsibility that Jesus had given to his ones in the beginning. Hence, the responsibility of Mary, of the apostles, of the first disciples comes from the same roots as the mission of the pilgrims of Međugorje.

Unfortunately, it is in the mentality of the faithful of our age to often live as separated from the placenta of life, separated from this environment that shapes the Church and that makes faith possible. Belonging to the Church becomes an object of imaginary statistics, of an administrative procedure, of image, of tribal or geographical belonging. In the Scripture, the Church is something else. The Church was born and has developed on the foundations of the Spirit that God has poured out on His own. In its nature, the Church is always Pentecostal. The living Spirit who always incarnates himself in the faithful and in their lives gives life to the Church. The Church was born on the day of Pentecost, is always born in the Spirit and becomes an outpouring of the Spirit on those who are one soul and one heart. The church cannot be other than Pentecostal. If it were not Pentecostal, it would be a *contradictio in se,* because the Church cannot exist only in this way. Can a human being exist without a body? If human beings must necessarily have a body to be humans, the more so must the Church possess what makes it to be Church.

Međugorje is a place of catechesis, a place of birth of the Church, a place of Pentecost. Catechesis is a global effort of the Church to make of all men disciples of Christ, to help them to believe that Jesus is the Son of God. When we read Mary's words addressed to the visionaries, "DEAR CHILDREN", everything becomes clear: Mary brings about her family and educates it.

Articles 13 to 17 of the Catechism of the Catholic Church speak about the structure of the Catechism; it is, in fact, the question of catechesis that indicates the very life of the Church.

In the catechesis, the Church is at the service of the Holy Spirit and so engenders its children. Catechesis is a style of life of the faithful in which they put themselves at the service of the life of the Church, while announcing Christ through a living witness, words and actions, like the apostles, and at the service of the Holy Spirit. That a faithful may be a member of the Church and that Church may live in him, he must – by the very nature of his mission – be a catechist as well as be catechized.

The catechesis – this blood circulation of the Church – consists in four essential steps in which the life of the Church can be situated:

1. The baptismal profession of faith. The church begins with the act of faith in Christ and with baptism. With the baptism, the faithful receives the Revelation and puts himself at the service of the Revelation through which

God addresses himself to men. In Međugorje, the living Revelation takes place and faith awakens.

2. The sacraments. God's salvation, accomplished once for all through Christ Jesus and the Holy Spirit, is made present in the sacred actions of the Church's liturgy, especially in the seven sacraments. This is why the catechesis in Međugorje leads necessarily towards the sacraments.

3. Faith is possible only in the accomplishment of the commandments and in a life according to the commandments. This is why the coming to Međugorje is not as important as the return home.

4. The Lord's Prayer. Faith is possible only in prayer and remains alive in prayer. (Cf.: *Lumen Gentium* 14, CEC ch. 13 to 17)

Dr. Richard Foley, a great friend of Međugorje deceased at the end of 2002, a Jesuit, a pioneer among the pilgrims, often repeated that there was only one message in Međugorje: PRAYER.

This vital catechetical context of the Church is recognizable in Međugorje from the very beginning. In Međugorje, we recognize the Church that is born, that lives, suffers and dies, just as the Lord. In Međugorje, we see the Pentecostal Church that Scriptures are talking about, the Pentecostal Church, which is Pentecostal today. In Međugorje the life of the Church of the first years after the Resurrection is recognizable, which is spoken of in the Acts of the Apostles.

Catechism (catechesis) is a mission, a responsibility and a style of life, of action and of witnessing of the faithful. True catechesis – see Mary! – is the way by which the Spirit of God is being incarnate in the life of the faithful. In this process the Church emerges and the mission of the faithful happens. It is precisely for this reason that some-body called pilgrimage *incarnate prayer or total prayer.* A pilgrim said to me: "My intelligence is useless to me, I can do nothing with it, but I climb Križevac and there, I stand, I sit... and I am fine".

How did the awareness of the mission and the respon-sibility spread in Međugorje?

If we look at the written testimonies about the events of Međugorje, we see that – in an unexplainable and mi-raculous way – somebody walks on the stage called Me-đugorje and distributes tasks. Tasks were given to the visionaries, their families, their neighbors, to priests and religious sisters, to the police, the army, the media, to the local authorities and men on highest functions, to people from near and from far. Many of them were called in a miraculous and surprising way. Tasks are distributed so far in all the parts of the world and to all those who hear about Međugorje.

Ivanka had said to Mirjana: *"Behold, Our Lady!"* After these words, their life changes definitively. When Vicka spoke about Our Lady to Marija and to Jakov, they imme-diately went on the Hill. Remember how the apostle An-drew catechizes his environment... (Cf.: Jn 1:40-42)

Jakov testifies that they asked the question: *"What is your name?" She* answered: *"I AM THE BLESSED VIRGIN MARY".* (Cf.: *At the Sources of Međugorje,* Darija Škunca Klanac, p. 84) The third day, Marija testi-fies, *"Our Lady told us: BE RECONCILED".*

That day, when they asked Our Lady: *"Will we be able to endure all this?"* Our Lady answered: *"YOU WILL, MY ANGELS".* Marinko Ivanković came with the children to help them, to protect and advise them. People arrived by the thousands; the Communists called them an *uncon-*

trollable crowd. Everything was at the service of the launching of the process.

The State authorities were drawn in and tested the power of the witness of the children, of the priests and of the faithful – the first pilgrims.

Fr. Jozo Zovko, the pastor, received the task: *"GO AND PROTECT THE CHILDREN"*.

Fr. Zrinko Čuvalo was pastor's assistant and the first priest to whom the visionaries came to give their report and testimony on the unusual events on Podbrdo. In a conversation that I personally had with Fr. Zrinko a few months before his illness and his death, Fr. Zrinko said: *"You see, I could say the same even today as concerns those children – the visionaries. Not only today but all this time I have been fighting against myself and I cannot be in the clear about what is happening with me, why, up to this day, those children have never interested me at all although everything happens through them. They are a medium, a bridge, and there is no crossing from one riverbank to the other except by that bridge. But you see, that bridge does not interest me at all and that is what amazes, what puzzles me.*

I shall, however, return on what I started to say, namely on what awoke me for the first time from that darkness which ensued, which was taking more and more possession of us – both Fr. Jozo and me.

What was the first light that flashed up in that darkness? It was neither what was occurring on the hill, nor the whiteness on Križevac, but a meeting with a woman. One morning, when I went to the church for the morning prayer and Mass, I saw in front of the church a woman who was waiting. She caught me by the sleeve with the request to make a confession. I told her to wait a little un-

til I open the church, but she insisted: "I would like to make a confession." *And I told her:* "But for God's sake, woman, don't you see, I'm going to open the church, can't you wait until after the morning prayer." *We were accustomed to praying the Laudes first, then, ten minutes before Mass, we would go out to hear confessions if there were any. Afterwards, we would start with Mass. But she continued even more:* 'I'd like to have it done right away. I'm in distress!" "All right then, if you insist", *I said. She knelt down trembling and shaking all over. I thought:* "Whatever is the matter? What is the big trouble?" *The woman made her confession, after which I invited her to my office where we had a talk, and where she left her written testimony. That is why I can speak about it now. The point is that this woman was sterile and that she had done everything to have a child. She made vows, she fasted, she went to different shrines, but nothing helped, she remained sterile although relatively young still. She had been married for approximately fifteen years. When she heard about the apparitions of Međugorje, she insulted Our Lady:* "What Our Lady! If she existed, she would have answered my prayers. How many shrines have I visited barefooted, how much have I fasted." *But the next Sunday she went to Mass and when she came to the church she hardly found courage to go in as if something had petrified her. Once in the church she was seized by anguish and fainted so that the other women had to lead her out of the church. Her husband took her home where she fainted again. In her testimony she said that, when she saw Our Lady's statue in the church she was simply blocked. When she came home she asked in the middle of the night to go and confess. Her husband did not let her go and disturb the Franciscans at this hour.*

The inner struggle of this woman was the first light for me in this darkness, a sign that God was at work notwith-standing my doubts and all what I said, because this was a sign, a sign of a true faith, which was for me more clear and more tangible than fire on the hill. You see: this sim-ple, apparently small thing enlightened me more than the hill, more than the fire on Crnica or the whiteness around the cross. This is what I wanted to say to describe my advancing in faith".

The moment, about which Fr. Zrinko testifies in the history of the action of God in Međugorje, was a moment of discernment of spirits and a moment when priests be-came aware of their mission. Priests recognized what they had to do and this woman clearly indicated where they were to go. Through Holy Sacraments, a believer answers the call of God. In Međugorje a practical catechesis hap-pens where the Holy Spirit is the Master and where Mary is the maidservant of the Lord.

As a priest and pastor, Fr. Jozo clearly distinguished the signs on the way. When he called the faithful to prayer, he answered to an inspiration of the Holy Spirit. In a conversation, he said: *"In these difficult days full of grace, I wanted that we begin to interiorise, to enter within ourselves, because all that was happening was there for us. I wanted for people to cease to extend the neck and to look only towards the children, that they cease to listen to what the children were going to say: where was Our Lady, what was Our Lady going to do, etc. I wanted to transmit the permanent call of God to conversion. People started to forget that they were per-sonally concerned, they stopped to receive and accom-plish tasks, and they had become simple observers, curi-ous spectators. I felt that my first task was to break people of this habit. How to do it? People had seen Jesus breaking and multiplying the bread, they heard him say to Lazarus: "Rise!" and saw him raise Lazarus, but they had started again to confuse the values while saying: "He is doing it by the power of Satan!" To avoid this happening to us, to make possible a real encounter with God, it was necessary for us to be purified, to be converted."*

The day of the first evening Mass in Međugorje, Fr. Jozo asked Fr. Zrinko to pray the rosary with the faithful, so that he may have time to prepare himself. This is how the Evening Prayer Program came about. In the need, in great crisis and tension that had arisen, one could only pray.

On one side was the communist system of the communist Yugoslavia with all its machinery, and on the other the faithful, the Church... Many people believe that the end of Communism started with the arrival of a Polish Pope and the beginning of Međugorje.

Fr. Jozo continues: *"In Holy Mass and Holy Sacraments, these curious people ceased being observers and became participants of the exceptional happenings, participants who pray. God guided all that. In the celebration of Holy Sacraments, many tears of repentance were shed, but also many tears of joy because of the grace of God."*

In these twenty-one years of the events of Međugorje, chroniclers, preachers and participants, observers and those who memorized the events continuously notice something that remains miraculous and unique for everyone: How is it possible that all occurred the way in which it occurred?

Events that nobody could either orchestrate or control progressed by an unforeseeable but regular way, as directed by the perfect baton of the Master of an orchestra.

Now, with the distance in time, somebody could say that the people triumphed, that the visionaries triumphed, that the faithful triumphed, that those or these triumphed. However, no one of them triumphed. In what would have Fr. Jozo Križić triumphed, who was imprisoned, who spent years in jail and who returned sick and died quickly afterwards? In what would have the parishioners triumphed?

Who are the winners in Međugorje? The victory is on two sides of the wire. Only the sacraments are victorious. The winners are only in the sacraments. The victory can be measured only by sacraments. Thus, if this Sunday somebody went to Mass, for confession and received Holy Communion, he is victorious today whatever side he was on in 1981. If somebody was among the triumphant victors in 1981, if he was on good side then and speaks about it today still, but on Sunday did not go for Mass and made no confession during the whole year, he is beaten and will remain beaten until he returns to the sacraments.

It is precisely on the footsteps of the sacraments that we observe the mission and the responsibility of the friends of Međugorje. Friends of Međugorje are visible only through the sacraments. By the sacraments will you recognize them. The measure of faith in Međugorje, and consequently the measure of friendship, are the sacraments. In Međugorje, the faithful never doubted about the direction to take. The genetic code of their faith contains the sacraments. Thus, Međugorje goes firmly with the Church and there is no other way. (Cf.: *Lumen Gentium* 11)

This is why I rejoice for two priests from Philadelphia, for priests from Vienna, for priests from Ireland who received their vocation in Međugorje. I rejoice for Irish converts who found in Međugorje the way towards faith. I rejoice for the couple from Chicago – people who were already divorced: they came almost by chance together on pilgrimage, and now they are together. I rejoice for an excellent businessman from Germany who gave up the great family business, who accompanies pilgrims to Međugorje, leads them towards the sacraments and builds churches in Russia. I rejoice for Marc from Munic who gave up alcohol, who accompanies pilgrims and carries Our Lady's medals on the Red Square in Moscow. I rejoice for a housewife from Dublin who nourished and comforted thousands of victims of the war in Croatia and Bosnia-Herzegovina.

The Acts of the Apostles in Chapter 2 does not forget to mention that all those who embraced faith had all in common. In faith, which is faithful to itself and its nature, the spiritual and the material intermingle. An Irish pilgrim said that she experienced the grace of faith and conversion when, exhausted and tired, she had met an attentive old woman who invited her to her house: she nourished her and shared with her the modest home of her family. How many people were touched when they had received a cup of fresh water and a nice word! They did not ask for more, and what they had received had nourished their body and their heart. In the middle of the year 1992, a group of pilgrims from Malawi came to Međugorje; I still remember cans and food, which they had brought to the displaced people. I accompanied them to a family. The pilgrims offered their gifts and people willingly accepted them. It was as when the Magi came to Bethlehem. Now that times are difficult in Malawi, will somebody give love for love?

In Međugorje, the natives and the hosts are pilgrims. Each pilgrim is a gift and an obligation. If we yield to temptation and look at everything from our personal perspective and our own interests, we will project on the pilgrims our problems and our interests. We will burden them with all the material and spiritual problems of this area, of this people and of our history. Such an attitude is like a contagious disease: it spreads unceasingly, and those who are in touch with it become ill. What a tragedy when a householder speaks to the pilgrims from England about the Second World War! Pilgrims come to Meðugorje as they went to Jesus. They do not want to contract diseases. They are sick and want to be healed. They want to eat when they are hungry, to drink when they are thirsty, and they want that the word of God be preached to them. The pilgrims who come have their needs and their interests that Gospa, the Queen of Peace, recognizes and because of which she calls them. We will be good hosts and good guides if we recognize the needs of the pilgrims that Our Lady had recognized, and if we answer in a creative way, in the Holy Spirit, unceasingly keeping in mind that we are at the service of the Church. Pilgrims should never be an object of our interests. Their interest and their ultimate desires can never be filled by us. Our common interest can be defined by only one word: CHURCH. Their interest and our interest can be carried out only within the framework of the Church. Jesus will give the blessing, which is called the Church, and he will not forget any need for the people. This is how I see the mission and the responsibility of the friends of Meðugorje, wherever they may be, here in the parish or at the other end of the world. The mission and the responsibility are always the same for all: it is the catechesis in which emerges the CHURCH.

Fr. Svetozar Kraljević, OFM

PART 5
DOCUMENTS AND EVALUATIONS

XX

REPORT OF PROFESSOR STOPAR LUDVIK, M.D.

Professor Ludvik is a Doctor of Neuropsychiatry and Psychotherapy, Professor of Theistic Parapsychology at the University, Maribor, Slovenia. This report is for the Parish of St. James, Međugorje, and the Office of the Bishop of Mostar.

Subject: Parapsychological events (June 24-25, 1981) associated with alleged first appearance of Virgin Mary to six visionaries (11 – 18 years old) at approximately 1800. Reportedly, these children see, listen to, and speak to Mary, who makes recommendations to them, admonishes them, and answers questions for them. The alleged visions last between 3 and 10 minutes.

Endeavor: Confirmation of that activity and determination of the meaning of the alleged phenomena by religious commission in Mostar.

I belong to the discipline of theistic parapsychology, which recognizes the possibility of transcendence.

Parapsychology, with its sister discipline paraphysics, is obliged to investigate such alleged phenomena, wherever they occur. The two disciplines also investigate reports of Christian mysticism, including the category claimed by charismatic mystics as "gifts of discernment."

In psychosomatic relations, the soul receives "impulses" from God or from Satan. It has been found, in seeking the origins or foundations of such phenomena, that 10 percent originate in or are influenced by everyday consciousness or awareness, and 90 percent begin in deep sub-consciousness.

The 10 percent or "everyday consciousness" is made up of reason, culture, intellect (corrected), age and experience, etc. The subconscious, which accounts for 90 percent of the phenomena, proceeds from – is made up of – intuition, inspiration, instinct, conscience ("the inner voice"), sentiment or animal spirits, etc.

CONCRETIZATION

The six visionaries of Međugorje claim they actually see the Virgin physically, in three dimensions. In such visions, visionaries have the conviction that they see a living person. Such are the subjective experiences (as noted above) that have allegedly been occurring for the last twenty-one months, daily around 18:00.

PSYCHOSOMATIC CONDITION OF THE VISIONARIES

Scientific and sociological tests, including (respectively) neuropsychiatric, medico-psychological, somatic, adolescent and young-adult profiles, lifestyle characteristics, and intelligence and educational standards, show the children to be absolutely normal and free from all psychopathological reactions.

OBJECTIVIZATION

Manipulation can be indicated only by medical hypnosis. However, the 10 percent "consciousness" category is excluded from this state of trance. And although the 90 percent "sub-consciousness" category is susceptible to hypnotic phenomena, the latter cannot produce unreal (i.e. nonexperienced) experiences or objective acts of such nature consistently over a 21-month period.

Drawing conclusions on other than fundamental and empirical evidence would produce unwarranted and fallacious statements, especially as they pertain to parapsychological phenomena. Therefore I ask that the Religious Commission of the Church Tribunal in Mostar be authorized to conduct a canonical investigation of the events reported at Međugorje, that its findings be critically assessed as theistic parapsychological phenomena, and that the possibilities of human manipulation and transcendental agency (the hand of God!) be determined.

(signed) STOPAR LUDVIK, Theistic Parapsychologist
Maribor, December 1982

(Dr. Stopar spent seven days in Međugorje incognito, studying and observing, before he made this report. He first went to Međugorje as a pilgrim, then stayed in Međugorje for six days, studying and observing. Observing all that happened, without disclosing to anyone who he was and what he was doing, Dr. Stopar talked to other pilgrims and to the visionaries. Dr. Stopar is also a member of the International Commission of Doctors-experts who investigate alleged miraculous healings at Lourdes, France.)

XXI

THE BISHOP'S STATEMENT

About the "Apparition" in Herzegovina

1. The public expects us to say something about the events in the parish of Međugorje, where six children claim Our Lady appears to them.

    When newspapermen write about this, with their atheistic convictions, it is to be expected that they will deny the truthfulness of what the children say. Their conviction that God does not exist extends as well to Mary. For believers, the way they write about it and condemn it, with absolutely no evidence, is unacceptable and offensive. The children, they say, are "talked into it."

2. Newspaper articles about the Faith, written by people in positions of power, in derogative and derisive terms, advance no evidence for their conclusions. Among their numerous insinuations about priests is their imputation that priests, "through underage children, assembled and trained them, with the knowledge of their parents... and have endeavored to persuade them that Our Lady appears to them in human form."

3. It is also untrue that Church authorities have preached against the events in Bijakovići, declaring them superstitious. We also deplore the fact that the Catholic Church in Herzegovina is falsely condemned in public for having political and deceitful intentions.

4. Generally, believers must admit the possibility of apparitions and miracles. Although we, as a believer,

do not deny Jesus Christ and the saints to do holy acts, we know that the Church is all but scrupulous before it makes a judgment about apparitions and miracles (e.g., Lourdes, Fatima, etc.).

5. Throughout history, some pious souls have claimed to see visions, but often these have been hallucinations or a highly subjective psychological experience, or even outright lies.

6. What can we say about what has happened at Bijakovići? It is certain that the children have not been "talked into" anything, and have not – certainly not by the Church – been encouraged to speak falsehoods. Everything indicates that the children are not lying. However, the most difficult question remains: Are the children undergoing subjective supernatural experiences?

7. When the Jews tried to silence the Apostles, according to the Acts of the Apostles, a teacher of the Law, highly regarded by all the people, Gamaliel, said to the Jewish assembly: "If their purpose or activity is human in its origins, they will destroy themselves. If, on the other hand, what they say comes from God, you will not be able to destroy them" (Acts 5:38 – 39).

This is our stand at present.

PAVAO ŽANIĆ Bishop of Mostar

(Glas Koncila, Aug. 16, 1981, p. 1)

XXII

DECLARATION OF THE BISHOPS' CONFERENCE IN ZADAR ON MEĐUGORJE

At the ordinary session of the Bishops' Conference in Zadar, Croatia, April 9-11, 1991, the following was adopted:

Declaration

"The Bishops, from the very beginning, have been following the events of Međugorje through the Bishop of the diocese (Mostar), the Commission of the Bishop (Mostar) and the Commission of the Bishops' Conference on Međugorje.

"On the basis of the investigations so far, it can not be affirmed that one is dealing with supernatural apparitions and revelations.

"However, the numerous gatherings of great numbers of the faithful from different parts of the world, who are coming to Međugorje prompted both by motives of belief and various other motives, do require attention and pastoral care – in the first place by the Bishop of the diocese and with him also of the other Bishops, so that both in Međugorje and in everything connected with it a healthy devotion to the Blessed Virgin Mary may be promoted in accordance with the teaching of the Church.

"For this purpose the Bishops will issue specially suitable liturgical-pastoral directives. Likewise, through their Commissions they will continue to keep up with and investigate the entire event in Međugorje."

The Bishops
In Zadar, April 10, 1991
(Published in *Glas Koncila* (Zagreb) May 5, 1991)

Comment and an explanation by Msgr. Franc Perko, Archbishop of Belgrade:

The bishops wrote: "non constat de supernaturalitate" (supernaturality is not established) and not: "constat de non supernaturalitate" (it is established that there is nothing supernatural). This is an enormous difference. The first formulation does not permit itself to be interpreted in a definitive way; it is open to further developments.

XXIII

CONGREGATIO PRO DOCTRINA FIDEI
ON MEDJUGORJE

Citta del Vaticano, Palazzo del S. Uffizio
Pr. No 154/81-06419
May 26, 1998

To His Excellency Mons. Gilbert Aubry,
Bishop of Saint-Denis de la Reunion

Excellency,

In your letter of January 1, 1998, you submitted to this
Dicastery several questions about the position of the Holy
See and of the Bishop of Mostar in regard to the so-called
apparitions of Medjugorje, private pilgrimages and the
pastoral care of the faithful who go there.

In regard to this matter, I think it is impossible to reply
to each of the questions posed by Your Excellency. The
main thing I would like to point out is that the Holy See
does not ordinarily take a position of its own regarding
supposed supernatural phenomena as a court of first
instance. As for the credibility of the "apparitions" in
question, this Dicastery respects what was decided by the
bishops of the former Yugoslavia in the Declaration of
Zadar, April 10, 1991: "On the basis of the investigations
so far, it can not be affirmed that one is dealing with
supernatural apparitions and revelations." Since the
division of Yugoslavia into different independent nations,

it would now pertain to the members of the Episcopal Conference of Bosnia-Herzegovina to eventually reopen the examination of this case, and to make any new pronouncements that might be called for.

What Bishop Peric said in his letter to the Secretary General of "Famille Chretienne", declaring: "My conviction and my position is not only 'non constat de supernaturalitate,' but likewise, 'constat de non supernaturalitate' of the apparitions or revelations in Medjugorje", should be considered the expression of the personal conviction of the Bishop of Mostar which he has the right to express as Ordinary of the place, but which is and remains his personal opinion.

Finally, as regards pilgrimages to Medjugorje, which are conducted privately, this Congregation points out that they are permitted on condition that they are not regarded as an authentification of events still taking place and which still call for an examination by the Church.

I hope that I have replied satisfactorily at least to the principal questions that you have presented to this Dicastery and I beg Your Excellency to accept the expression of my devoted sentiments.

Archbishop Tarcisio Bertone

*****

("Congregation for the Doctrine" is presided over by Cardinal Ratzinger, now Pope Benedict XVI)

This is the summary of the letter:

The declarations of the Bishop of Mostar reflect his personal opinion.

One is directed to the declaration of Zadar, which leaves the door open to future investigations. In the meanwhile, private pilgrimages with pastoral accompaniment for the faithful are permitted.

A new commission could eventually be named.

In the meanwhile, all Catholics may go as pilgrims to Medjugorje.

XXIV

STATEMENT ON THE TESTS PERFORMED ON THE VISIONARIES

- INSTITUTE FOR THE FIELD LIMITS OF SCIENCE-INNSBRUCK (INSTITUT FUR GRENZGEBIETE DER WISSENSCHAFT (IGW) – INNSBRUCK)
- CENTER FOR STUDY AND RESEARCH ON PSYCHO-PHYSIOLOGY OF STATES OF CONSCIOUSNESS – MILANO
- EUROPEAN SCHOOL OF HYPNOTIC PSYCHOTHERAPY AMISI OF MILAN
- PARAPSYCHOLOGY CENTER OF BOLOGNA

On April 22-23, 1998 at the Casa Incontri Cristiani (House of Christian Encounters) of Capiago-Como, of the Dehonian Fathers a psychophysiological and psychodiagnostic research took place on subjects

Ivan Dragičević,
Marija Pavlović Lunetti,
Vicka Ivanković,

who are commonly known as visionaries of the Medugorje group.

This research allows certain considerations: Since 1981 these subjects have had and still have some experiences that are defined as apparitions/visions of Our Lady.

In this center we have verified that such experiences provoke modifications of some measurable biological parameters.

The above subjects with full freedom and with an attitude of collaboration full liberty submitted to the following tests:

- complete case history,
- medical case history,
- MMPI, EPI, MHQ; Tree test, Person test, Raven Matrixes, Rorschach Test, Hand test,
- neurological visit,
- computerized polygraph (GSR; PERIPHERAL CARDIAC ACTIVITIES; PNEUMOGRAPHY 1-2)

during the apparitional experience and during the mediated hypnotic recall of the same apparitional experience:

- dynamic registration according to Holter of arterial pressure
- dynamic registration according to Holter Electrocardio-graphic (ECG)/respiratory
- pupillary reflexes (photomotor) and winking reflex
- video takes
- photographs

The results will be made public only after the complete analysis of the data and the completion of certain aspects of the research.

The coordinators of the research
E Andreas Resch
Dr. Giorgio Cagliardi

The following members of the above listed Institutes and Centers participated in the research:

Andreas Resch, theologian and psychologist; Giorgio Gagliardi, psychophysiologist; Marco Margnelli, psychophysiologist; Virginio Nava, psychiatrist; Luigi Ravagnati, neurologist; Mario Cigada, oculist psychotherapist; Giovanni Li Rosi, gynecologist psychotherapist; Marianna Bolko, psychiatrist; Gaetano Perriconi, internist; Gianfranco Fattori, neurophysiologist; Gabriella Raffaelli, scientific secretary; Fiorella Gagliardi, assistant community secretary.

Capiago, April 23, 1998

NB: The initiative for this investigation was undertaken by the parish office of Međugorje in agreement with the visionaries.

PUBLISHER:

INFORMATIVNI ✝ CENTAR

mir

M E Đ U G O R J E

www.medjugorje.hr
e-mail: medjugorje-mir@medjugorje.hr

FOR THE PUBLISHER:
Fr. Ivan Sesar

PREPARED FOR THE PRINT BY:
Jozo Kraljević